# Contents

# Contents

# Foreword

There is no industry quite like IT: in the 21st century we all depend on technology everyday.

For those who work in the industry these are exciting times, as there are a huge variety of careers available, all with the potential of positively impacting modern society.

Those with a creative bent will design the next generation of user interfaces and interactive web pages; the logical thinkers will develop ever more powerful applications with their programming prowess; individuals with an eye for detail will manage the projects of tomorrow; deep thinkers will create the next generation of artificial intelligence systems; gregarious individuals will provide the support necessary to continue the process of demystifying IT and opening it up to all.

These career paths, and those we haven't room to mention, will require the recognised professionals of the future.

The British Computer Society (BCB) is dedicated to the aim of making IT a professionally recognised pursuit. Why? Because it's difficult to think of anything in the 21st century that has not been made more effective, quicker, or easier because of computers, and this means that we often have our literal lives in the hands of those who design, program, maintain and develop systems. It's in the interest of society as a whole that those people should be recognised as competent – a goal the BCS is pursuing.

An IT workforce of skilled professionals is achieved by the acquisition and maintenance of the right qualifications. As the main IT membership organisation in the United Kingdom, the

BCS contributes to this through the industry-recognised qualifications, from end-user qualifications such as European Computer Driving Licence® to the world-renowned Information Systems Examinations Board certificates, which cover many areas of practitioner expertise.

The BCS is committed to encouraging diversity in the IT workplace, too. Currently there are too few women in the profession, which has led to a lack of specific skills sets – the Society want all to be invited into **the profession of the 21st century**.

Enjoy your read, and remember that the BCS is here to provide support at every stage of your IT career. For more information and resources please visit www.bcs.org/careers.

*David Clarke*
*Chief Executive*
*The British Computer Society*

# Acknowledgements

For granting permission to reprint copyright material, I would like to thank *Computer Weekly* and *Computing*.

With two small children at home (Ben and Jack), writing a book is never easy. While they gladly offered to help their daddy, my publishing deadline meant that I had to decline their kind offer. So it is my wife, Anne, that I must thank as it was she who supervised the kids while I was writing this book.

# Introduction

## IS THIS THE JOB FOR YOU?

- Do I have an interest in computing and IT?

- Do I possess sufficient IT skills to enter the IT industry?

- Am I prepared to learn new skills to meet the changing demands on the IT profession?

- Do I have a flexible and professional approach to work?

- Do I want to work in computer gaming, sales or IT training?

- Do I want to be an IT user or do I want to be an IT practitioner, actively involved in building, testing and implementing IT systems?

- What are my career aspirations? Do I want to specialise in a specific IT area or be a good 'all-rounder'?

- What are my financial aspirations? Do I accept the Internet-boom is over and that I am unlikely to become an Internet millionaire overnight?

- Do I have the right aptitude to succeed in IT? Communication and management skills are now as important as IT skills.

IT is far from dead. It is more important than ever and it is changing. Carly Fiorina, Chief Executive HP (Hewlett Packard), *Computing*, 16 October 2003

1

Information technology (IT) has, quite simply, changed the way we live and work. We are now fast approaching a time when everyone and everything will be connected to the network. The online generation of 'intelligent devices' is now upon us – the list already includes mobile phones, cars, cameras, games, personal desktop assistants (PDAs), petrol pumps and all manner of medical devices.

Everyone it seems uses IT – particularly Internet technology as a means to improve their health, their business or their leisure time. IT now allows people, either as users or as IT professionals, to work from anywhere – at home, on the road, or in the office. This not only improves our work-life balance, it also helps industry save millions every year by reducing costs.

The key to success in today's IT profession is establishing and maintaining a good range of IT skills. Luckily, many UK employers such as BMW and Orange recognise this and are actively helping their IT staff improve their skills through a range of programmes, such as the Modern Apprenticeship programme (more details on education and training opportunities can be found in Chapter 8). In many respects, opportunities for new entrants into IT are high – they can offer a good range of IT skills and, by having more realistic salary expectations than more experienced IT professionals, are ultimately more marketable.

## How to use this book

This book will give you an up-to-date insight into computing and IT: how it has developed into the lucrative and rewarding industry it is today and how it will develop in the future. The early chapters of the book will provide you with general information on the IT industry and its structure. Chapters 2 and 3 describe both the core activities of the industry and its allied professions. Chapters 5 and 6 cover the jobs available within those sectors and how you should set out to achieve your goal – a career in computing and IT. Included in the book are a number of company profiles that examine some of the major employers within the industry and case studies of their employees. These case studies relate to real people who work in the IT industry and describe what IT employees *really* do at work, how they got there and what you need to do if you want to work in a similar role. The latter chapters of the book provide information on the qualifications and training opportunities available and where you can study for them.

This book can only give you a general guide to the many opportunities available for training and employment within the IT industry. If you follow the advice within it, however, you will be able to use your time well in planning a career in IT. Whatever you plan to do, be confident – plan for success!

# 1

# Computing and information technology

Today we live in a society where we have access to an enormous amount of information from all over the world. In fact, there are very few places on the planet where information *cannot* be accessed. Thanks to computing and IT, we have relatively simple access to huge amounts of information in seconds. Indeed, thanks to massively powerful computers that can hold huge amounts of information, combined with high-speed telecommunications networks, electronic mail (e-mail), the Internet and multimedia technologies (digital imaging and sound), the world is a much smaller place.

However, the industry is not just a place where degree-laden university students can unleash their skills; the widespread use of PCs in business has created a huge number of career openings for those people who use computing and IT in their workplace. The potential market for people with IT skills is larger than you might think; in total, it is estimated that the UK spent more than £65 billion on IT during 2003 – an average of £2,546 for every employee.

# A BRIEF HISTORY

Computing and IT is breaking new technological barriers all the time, but it is nothing new. The first computers were developed during the 1940s, following years of research in both the UK and the USA.

Early commercial computers were so large they would often fill an entire room; they also consumed huge amounts of power and were very expensive to build. So great was the investment required, many experts believed only a few dozen computers would *ever* be needed.

With the development of the transistor, computers, still relatively expensive, began to take up less room and consume less power. Soon after came the development of the integrated circuit, which allowed thousands of transistors and other electrical components to be 'printed' onto a piece of silicon – the 'silicon chip' as we know it today. Mass production and sophisticated manufacturing techniques have since allowed the power of the silicon chip to be produced in large numbers at little cost. Today, almost all electronic equipment contains a 'microchip', from a small camera to the largest commercial computer systems.

If you are seriously considering a career within the IT industry, then good news is on the way. A number of surveys are now showing the first significant demand for IT staff for nearly three years.

# EMERGING TECHNOLOGIES

Application development, database management and communication systems are nothing new; many of them have been established within the IT industry for several decades. Naturally, many new entrants into the profession will work in these areas – this is fine: after all, they do encompass popular technologies such as TCP/IP, UNIX, SQL, Oracle, Microsoft, C++ and Java.

However, the IT industry, just like many others, has had to reinvent itself to cope with the ever-changing demands from a global economy. Innovation and re-engineering is the name of the game in today's IT industry, partly due to the need for IT companies to reduce their operating costs through system integration and process innovation, but also because there is a need to build something that has never been needed before.

Knowing what is happening within the IT world provides significant benefits if you are seeking employment within it; for one thing, it may help you decide who you want to work for and what you want to do when you get there; secondly, interviewers often throw in a few general questions about future trends within the industry just to see how many applicants express a genuine desire to work with IT and to articulate that desire in a comprehensive and coherent way. Table 1.1 gives a brief summary of some of the new and exciting technologies that are being introduced into the IT industry, some more quickly than others – watch this space!

# E-COMMERCE

E-commerce (a shortened form of electronic commerce) is a term used to describe trading over a network. Despite the term being coined from the jargon associated with the Internet revolution, it is nothing new, having its roots in electronic data interchange (EDI), which became popular in the 1980s. Today, however, e-commerce describes the operations and systems supporting the buying and selling of goods over the Internet.

E-commerce has become popular as it removes many, if not all, of the limiting factors associated with traditional retail operations, namely, time, space and shop location. A 'shop' on the Internet has unlimited space and can trade 24 hours a day, seven days a week. Equally, there are no limits to the amount of products a shop can offer. For instance, Amazon.com offers more than 4.7 million books; imagine a bookshop with 4.7 million books in stock! Admittedly, this is an unfair comparison as Amazon does not stock the books, but orders them on demand.

**Table 1.1**   Emerging technologies

| Technology | Description | Usage and benefit |
|---|---|---|
| WiFi | Wireless fidelity | A wireless network protocol used to support mobile computing applications. Using a laptop in a hotel foyer to connect to the Internet without a LAN connection is a typical example of wireless computing. |
| RFID | Electronic bar-code tagging | Retail sector. Clothes are 'tagged' during manufacture. Designed to prevent theft from shops. |
| Digital encryption/ Internet security | Anti-virus software; network security | Reducing threat from malicious hackers; reducing cost of computer fraud. |
| Grid computing | Massively distributed computing | Phenomenal processor power available through linked computer systems. Used in large research projects such as those within the space and pharmaceutical industries. |
| Chip and pin | 'Smart' credit cards | Transaction security in the retail sector. |
| Biometrics | Using characteristics of the human body to generate a unique identification | Fraud prevention. Used in conjunction with health sector computing. Examples include retina scan, fingerprint identification and voice identification. |

# WHAT'S IN IT FOR ME?

Computing and IT is now used in just about every walk of life, from the demanding worlds of science, medicine, defence, politics and business to the more relaxing pastimes of recreation, entertainment and personal development. Figure 1.1 shows where and how computing and IT can be used within the key industry sectors. It is by no means the complete picture, but it should help in deciding your route into computing and IT, whether you intend to become a user of IT or a practitioner.

Clearly, one of the key decisions you will need to make in order to achieve your career goals and aspirations concerns

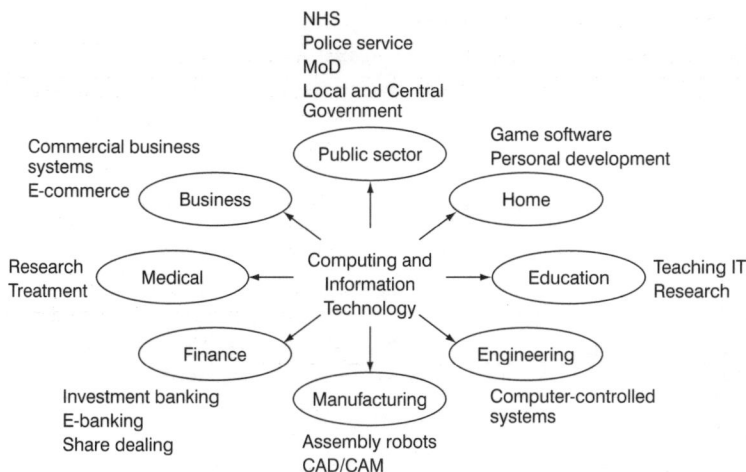

**Figure 1.1** How computing and IT is used in key industry sectors

the role you would like to perform in the industry. At its simplest, you have two options: to be an IT user (often referred to as an 'end-user') or to be a practitioner of IT.

Users of IT, who represent a huge proportion of the working population, rarely possess an IT degree; indeed many do not possess any degree at all. Business users, as any business or systems analyst will tell you, are vital in the development and implementation of business computing systems. Why? Simply because they understand how their business works, both from a business process perspective (such as how a customer order is processed between departments) and from a systems perspective (such as the IT systems they must use to support their business processes).

IT users will use all manner of IT systems to support their business processes; some maybe stand alone, such as Microsoft Excel; other systems may be shared amongst the team, department or even across the organisation over a network.

For those of you who aspire to a career in IT but do not possess a degree or even A-levels, starting your career as a user of IT is a good bet. With suitable and relevant IT training, your business skills combined with your IT skills should enable you to move into the organisation's IT department, usually in a junior support or programming role. Don't be disheartened: it may take time, but I know of many senior IT professionals earning well over £70,000 a year who started their IT careers in the company postroom. I kid you not...

# IT SKILLS AND SALARIES

## Top IT skills

The IT industry can be a fickle thing and having the right skills at the right time is often the key to success. With the industry changing at an alarming pace, keeping up with the latest skills is often the greatest challenge for many IT professionals, especially contractors, who normally have to fund their own skills training. The skills most in demand within the IT profession have remained fairly consistent, with UNIX and SQL leading the pack within IT companies (see Table 1.2).

## The IT contract market

The growth in contract jobs has been matched with a steady rise in the number of software houses requiring specialist or short-term skills to meet project deadlines, a greater number of financial institutions and many more opportunities in the public sector. Table 1.3 shows a breakdown of IT jobs within the contract market by industry sector.

## Working within an industry sector

In an ever-changing IT industry, flexibility is the key to establishing and maintaining a long and successful career in computing and IT. Experience has shown that the area in which you start your IT career bears little resemblance to the eventual path your career will follow. The IT industry is about computers, but it is also about *people*. Having a flexible attitude to where you work and what you do can often mean the difference between success and failure. While there will always be a need for specialists in the industry, if you possess skills that are in demand in more than one industry sector, you should have a fairly secure and rewarding career. Table 1.4 should give you an idea of the main areas within IT where you could work.

**Table 1.2**   The top 25 software skills in demand

| Skill | Position | | Category |
|---|---|---|---|
| | **(July–Sep 2003)** | **(July–Sep 2002)** | |
| SQL | 1 | 1 | Database descriptor language |
| Unix | 2 | 3 | Operating system |
| Oracle | 3 | 4 | Relational database |
| C++ | 4 | 2 | Programming language |
| Microsoft Office | 5 | 8 | PC utilities |
| Java | 6 | 7 | Application development environment |
| C | 7 | 6 | Programming language |
| Windows NT | 8 | 5 | PC operating system |
| Visual Basic | 9 | 9 | Programming language |
| SQL Server | 10 | 10 | Relational database |
| XML | 11 | 11 | File-handling language |
| Windows 2000 | 12 | 20 | PC operating system |
| .net | 13 | 25 | Microsoft Web-development environment |
| SAP | 14 | 12 | Finance and accounting software |
| ASP | 15 | 15 | Web-based development |
| HTML | 16 | 14 | Web page development |
| Microsoft Exchange | 17 | 24 | PC-based electronic mail |
| Solaris | 18 | 16 | PC operating system |
| Microsoft Access | 19 | 18 | PC-based relational database |
| UML | 20 | 19 | Programming language |
| TCP/IP | 21 | 17 | Network protocol |
| Object-oriented system | 22 | 21 | Application design and development |
| Embedded systems | 23 | 13 | Programs used within other components, such as flight navigation systems, missile systems |
| Linux | 24 | 27 | Operating system |
| C# (C-sharp) | 25 | 47 | Programming language |

(Source: *SSP/Computer Weekly Quarterly Survey of Appointments Data and Trends*)

## Top IT roles

There are marked differences in current demand for IT specialists compared to the job market of the late 1990s.

**Table 1.3**  Breakdown of IT jobs for contractors by industry sector

| Industry sector | % change from Q1 2002 to Q2 2003 |
| --- | --- |
| Electronics | –0.1 |
| Software | 15.9 |
| Finance | 30.3 |
| Retail | –12.3 |
| Media | 34.8 |
| Manufacturing | –10.2 |
| Public sector | 26.5 |

(Source: *SSP/Computer Weekly Quarterly Survey of Appointments Data and Trends*)

**Table 1.4**  Breakdown of IT jobs by industry sector

| Industry sector | % change from Q2 2002 to Q2 2003 |
| --- | --- |
| Electronics | –8.5 |
| Software | 1.3 |
| Finance | 10.6 |
| Retail | –0.1 |
| Media | 3.9 |
| Manufacturing | –20.8 |
| Public sector | 1.8 |

(Source: *SSP/Computer Weekly Quarterly Survey of Appointments Data and Trends*)

One major change affecting the nature of IT recruitment is the outsourcing of IT roles to offshore companies. Development costs in the UK are considerably greater than in countries such as India because of the high salaries and daily rates given in earlier years to IT professionals in the UK; such costs in offshore companies are a fraction of those in the UK. While falls in demand have been fairly even across all types of IT employment categories, jobs for Web specialists fell more than other categories, by 80 per cent. Table 1.5 shows the percentage change in demand for IT roles between 2002 and 2003.

## What salary can I expect?

Salaries on offer within the IT industry still reflect a cautious and conservative approach to the years ahead, with pay for

**Table 1.5**   Change in demand by job category

| Job title | % Change in demand from Q2 2002 to Q3 2003 |
|---|---|
| All jobs | –47 |
| Management | –34 |
| Development | –50 |
| Programmers | –58 |
| PC support | –34 |
| Technical support | –36 |
| Software engineering | –59 |
| Database | –55 |
| Networking | –40 |
| Operations | –47 |
| Web specialists | –80 |

(Source: *SSP/Computer Weekly Quarterly Survey of Appointments Data and Trends*)

permanent IT staff rising on average by 1 per cent over the past few years. Ironically, while salaries for IT directors and managers dropped considerably in some sectors, average salaries for systems developers and programmers went up by between 2 and 3 per cent over the same period.

Table 1.6 provides an idea of what sort of salaries to expect in the main job areas within IT, at the time of writing. Don't forget, these figures are based on the 'transfer-value'

**Table 1.6**   Salaries

| Job title | Average salary |
|---|---|
| IT director | £72,272 |
| Management/systems consultant | £61,248 |
| Operations manager | £46,256 |
| Database administrator | £36,756 |
| Operator | £23,609 |
| Programmer | £26,675 |
| Systems analyst | £31,394 |
| Systems programmer | £32,810 |
| Web designer | £30,847 |
| PC support analyst | £19,073 |

(Source: *SSP/Computer Weekly Quarterly Survey of Appointments Data and Trends*)

of existing, experienced IT professionals, so the starting salaries for a first job will be considerable lower. Having said that, there are many London-based IT consultancy companies that are more than willing to pay over £25,000 to attract graduates in any discipline into their own training and development programme.

## Is a professional qualification really necessary?

The IT world remains undecided on what makes the best employees. Degree students possess many skills that are still seen as important to many employers, such as team working, communication and problem solving. Degrees also provide students with many general IT skills, allowing them to be more employable within different IT disciplines.

Entering the IT industry with just programming skills (through a certified Microsoft training programme, for example) *will* provide you with much needed skills in the short-term, but you might suffer from a lack of awareness in many other areas which you might need later on in your career, such as systems analysis, project management or financial analysis.

# 2

# The structure of the IT industry

The IT profession, as with many long-established professions, has numerous facets and specialist fields within which IT professionals operate. There are, however, three fundamental sectors: hardware, software and professional services. It is in these three sectors that the majority of IT careers will be found, as they provide the key IT skills and services to organisations requiring IT expertise; see Figure 2.1.

On a global scale companies are continually seeking to gain commercial advantage by adopting new technology. As a result, there has been a phenomenal rise in other industry sectors that have a strong affinity to IT, namely media and telecommunications; this combination has given rise to a new sector, referred to as technology, media and telecommunications (TMT). Some of the most successful organisations in the UK are found in the TMT sector, which is good news for anyone seeking a career in IT.

## IT HARDWARE, SOFTWARE AND SERVICES

The hardware, software and services sector is the one that employs the most people in the IT industry, and can offer the most opportunities for new entrants into the profession. Its size

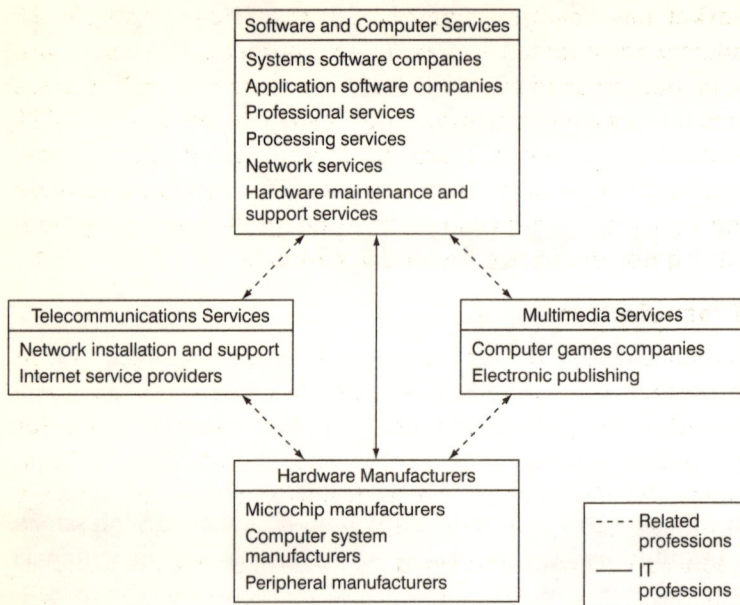

**Figure 2.1** IT sectors and services

and importance in terms of employment potential means that this sector is an area you should consider very carefully before deciding on any specific career path.

## IT hardware

Despite the boom in software, computer hardware is still a substantial area within the IT industry.

---

**FACT FILE**

The billionth PC was shipped in April 2002. The two billionth is expected to be delivered by early 2008.

---

During the early days of computing, the computer industry was dominated by a few huge companies, such as IBM and ICL, which were in fact hardware suppliers. The hardware market has changed significantly since then, and the IT industry has adopted a more 'open' approach. Customers are no longer forced to buy their computer hardware and software from the same manufacturer – they can go to any number of IT vendors. As a result, many hardware manufacturers now employ 'open' standards for chip design, computer interfaces and networking, allowing them to integrate their equipment with equipment from other manufacturers.

## IT manufacture

Computers, regardless of shape, size or cost rely upon silicon chips for their operation. As the demand for even more powerful computers increases, so too will the need for specialists capable of designing and manufacturing them. Almost 90 per cent of the high-performance chips found within large mid-range and mainframe computers are produced by Japanese-owned companies, such as Fujitsu and Mitsubishi, while the circuits found within most PCs are produced largely by American manufacturers such as Intel and Motorola.

It is worth remembering that careers in computer system manufacture involve a great deal more than just designing and testing integrated circuits. All computer systems are worthless unless there is some means of entering data into them and retrieving information from them. Every computer system therefore requires input and output devices, called peripherals, which include printers, display screens and storage devices (disks and tapes). There may also be networking and telecommunications equipment attached to the computer to allow information to be routed to another computer anywhere around the globe. Computer peripherals are manufactured throughout the world, including the UK and the rest of Europe.

### Career prospects

Computer hardware manufacturers can offer many highly skilled careers that cover every aspect of the manufacturing process, from design to distribution. While these companies seek to employ highly skilled professionals, there are always opportunities at more junior levels for people with fewer qualifications. It is often the case that a basic understanding of electronics and physics is all that is required for many of the 'entry-level' opportunities within this area as most, if not all, of the manufacturers have their own specific training and education programmes to develop expertise within the company. For example, IBM supports the NVQ programme, which provides on-the-job training and accreditation.

### Qualifications required

If you want to enter the areas of computer manufacture such as microprocessor design and digital electronic technology at a professional level, you will normally require as a minimum, education to A-level standard in subjects such as electronics, maths and computing. Even then, you will always face competition from those who have gained a degree in a relevant subject, such as computer science, digital electronics, and manufacturing and computing. Many of the larger computer manufacturers have extremely good graduate training programmes, and so can take graduates on in *any* discipline – yet more competition for those without a degree, unfortunately.

If you want to enter this field at an 'entry' level, in a support and administration role as opposed to a design and construction role, you will often need no more than a GCSE-level of education. What is important is having an *active* interest in computer design and manufacture and the ability to learn new skills. For example, the following list of skills would be considered very worthwhile for a junior position in computer design and manufacture:

- an interest in electronics, especially digital electronics;

- an interest in building, customising and fixing computers;

- an understanding of 'low-level' computer programming;

- the ability to reason rationally and logically, and good mathematical skills;

- the ability to understand and communicate technical issues effectively.

# IBM UK

IBM UK is a subsidiary of the IBM Corporation, which is one of the world's largest suppliers of information technology hardware, software, solutions and services. IBM is truly a worldwide IT company, providing solutions to customers in over 130 countries. Within the UK, IBM has sites at more than 25 locations, including Basingstoke, Bedfont Lakes, Greenock, Hursley, London, Portsmouth, Manchester and Warwick.

IBM's main activities include:

- manufacturing;

- development and support for computer software and hardware;

- software and consultancy services;

- Internet development and electronic trading services.

All the manufacturing undertaken by IBM in the UK is performed at their Greenock site in Scotland. IBM employs more than 3,000 people there in a wide variety of manufacturing and technical roles, ranging from high-volume assembly to IT management.

IBM Greenock is responsible for the development, manufacture and support of PCs for the European, Middle Eastern and African markets, and is the only site within IBM worldwide where design, manufacture and support are completely integrated. It employs over 250 overseas staff who manage customers' order from manufacture to delivery. This is carried out for 76 countries in 17 different languages. One of the most popular IBM products, the award-winning IBM ThinkPad, is manufactured entirely at Greenock.

*Qualifications required*

IBM accepts graduates from many disciplines, ranging from scientific and computing areas to the arts. As you would expect from a company with such a wide range of career options, IBM can offer employment at all levels, and for the more technical positions it welcomes graduates with a Master's degree. Having operations throughout the world, it is particularly keen to recruit IT professionals with language skills as well as technical skills. IBM regularly advertises at recruitment fairs and exhibitions throughout the year.

## INTEL IRELAND LTD

Intel Ireland is a subsidiary of the massive Intel Corporation, one of the market leaders in microprocessor design and manufacture. It is one of the largest IT companies to invest in Ireland, with over $1 billion invested in their Ireland operation.

Intel's manufacturing complex in County Kildare is the company's sole manufacturing centre for Europe, with four factories on-site. The company directly employs over 2,800 people, with another 800 people being employed on-site by other service companies.

Intel's main activities include:

- manufacture of semiconductor products (eg Pentium processor);

- manufacture of PC motherboards;

- manufacture of PCs and servers for leading computer vendors;

- PC maintenance and repair.

*Qualifications required*

Over a third of Intel employees are graduates. Owing to the wide-ranging skills used within the company, graduates are recruited from a number of disciplines, such as electronic engineering, mechanical engineering, computer science and information technology. As you would expect from a company whose operations are widespread, Intel can offer employment at all levels within the company: as a minimum, it recruits entry-level employees with five passes on their Leaving Certificate (the Irish equivalent of A levels).

Intel readily accepts 'on-spec' CVs for current and future positions – these are scanned electronically and stored on its recruitment database. Should a vacancy arise (Intel is currently recruiting heavily) the database is searched and a shortlist drawn up.

## Systems software

This area concerns the programs and utilities that control the operation of computers and the hardware devices attached to them (such as disk drives, tape units, monitors, printers and plotters). Collectively, these programs and utilities are referred to as the 'operating system'.

Working within systems software, for example as a Microsoft Certified Engineer, will mean maintaining the software infrastructure that supports the rest of the business. Typically, that will mean installing, configuring and maintaining operating systems (such as Windows 2000) or any number of software utility programs that help monitor, identify and resolve system faults.

## Applications software

Without applications software, the most powerful computers in the world are of little use to anyone – it is software that provides business users with the applications they need to trade and compete successfully in the marketplace. The majority of this software provides business users with the capability to retrieve, manipulate and store business information quickly and easily (business people are not computer experts).

Application software can be designed to run for one user on a PC, such as a database or word-processing package, or it can be designed to run for hundreds of users on large computer systems, where the application software might run the stock control system or the company's Web site.

Typical examples of application software used within business would include:

- e-commerce applications;
- billing and payroll systems;
- stock-control systems;
- financial accounts packages;
- call-centre/customer service systems.

## Professional services

As the number of applications, technologies and strategies developed by the IT industry increases, so too does the number of options available to business. For instance, what computer platforms should the business use to develop or expand its IT capability? How can the organisation protect its IT systems against the threats posed by hackers and computer viruses?

There are, of course, hundreds of other questions that organisations might want answers to (what software to buy is a popular one). None of these questions can be answered easily without understanding the organisation's specific business requirements – both in the short and in the long term. It is the role of IT consultants to help business managers understand how best they can use IT.

Professional services companies (IT consultancy organisations) provide their clients with skilled consultants to help them design, build and deploy new IT systems or for strategic advice. Most companies in this sector will therefore concentrate on providing some or all of the following: independent advice, system design and development, testing, implementation, and help-desk services.

## Processing services

This category provides business with specific computing services, such as processing monthly payroll information. Bureau companies provide a useful service to organisations that do wish to invest huge sums of money in computer systems for which they only have a limited use.

## The software development process

There is never a shortage of business problems that can be solved by the use of computer software, which is why a career within software development can be such an interesting one. When writing business software, it is crucial that you first understand the needs and requirements of the business and are able to identify the technical solution necessary to solve the problems. This is just the start of a lengthy process that begins with a business requirement and ends with a delivered computer solution – it is called the 'systems development lifecycle' (SDLC) (see Appendix 2). Many roles within the IT industry are related to one or more components of the SDLC.

*Career prospects*

There are very good opportunities for people wanting to work in the software and services sector; programmers continue to remain in demand at all levels from junior programmers working for local government to software development consultants working for the large multinational companies. If you like programming or are technically minded, then a career working for the systems and application software companies seems an obvious choice. Consultancy companies, while requiring technical skills, employ people who can also communicate and build a trusting relationship with their (fee-paying) clients.

If you want to walk straight into a consultancy role with one of the major professional service companies (eg Fujitsu, EDS, LogicaCMG, IBM or Deloitte), you will, without doubt, need a good degree. If the employer also has a graduate training programme, you will not necessarily need a degree in a computing subject – it will train you for whatever role you are best suited to.

# CAP GEMINI ERNST & YOUNG

Cap Gemini Ernst and Young (CGEY) is one of the world's largest consultancy and outsourcing suppliers, employing over 50,000 people worldwide. Cap Gemini was founded over 20 years ago by the merger of three computer services and consulting companies: CAP, Gemini Computer Services and Sogeti. In May 2000, Cap Gemini, Gemini Consulting and Ernst & Young formed CGEY, creating one of the world's leading global management and IT consultancy companies. You may think that CGEY is a US-owned company, but CGEY is in fact European-owned and its stock trades on the Paris stock exchange.

CGEY provides a broad range of services, which can be organised into five main areas:

1.  information technology consulting;

2.  systems outsourcing;

3.  software transformation;

4.  systems management (outsourcing);

5.  local professional services (undertaken by Sogeti).

## *Employment opportunities*

To work at a professional level within CGEY you will need a degree, although this can be in any subject. Candidates will be expected to sit an aptitude test as part of the recruitment process. Entry into this level *is* possible without a degree if candidates possess at least 18 months' experience in a particular IT field. As with many large companies, there are 'entry-level' opportunities for people who do not possess a degree; these are mainly based around providing a 'help-desk' support role for the desktop environment within the company (PCs, Windows, etc). CGEY does not take people on straight from school.

# 3

# Allied professions

## TELECOMMUNICATIONS SERVICES

The telecommunications services sector covers the many areas surrounding the transmission of different types of signals, such as speech, data and images. While most people might loosely call this telecommunications, it is much more than that: managing not only the building and running of the networks, but also the provision of services such as electronic commerce and electronic messaging systems.

### Telecommunications companies

Many of the larger telecommunications companies operating today were originally established to provide and support the public telephone system or to provide telecommunications services to business. Today, little has changed, with the exception that all telecommunications companies can now compete in almost all markets. With the greater use of digital technologies and high-speed networks, the ability to reach these new markets has increased tremendously and opportunities for employment are high.

Alongside developing new business areas using the Internet, telecommunications companies are leading the way in making available existing business technologies for home and personal use, such as high-speed broadband telephone lines and wireless technology. A subset of this sector comprises a number of companies that allow other companies and individuals access to their Internet network. These companies are known as Internet service providers (ISPs) and typically provide Web-hosting, content management and e-mail services for their customers. BT and Cable & Wireless are big players in this market, and despite the downturn in the demand for ISPs, there are still many other smaller ISPs doing very well.

## BT PLC

BT is one of world's leading telecommunications companies, whose principal activity is the supply of local, long-distance and international telecommunications services and equipment in the UK. Employing over 100,000 people, it is one of the largest companies in Europe.

Over recent years, the telecommunications sector has been a major casualty in the downturn in growth of Internet services. However, the market has stabilised, with the long overdue rationalisation and consolidation of many of the smaller ISPs, leaving BT once more in a dominant position.

Most people recognise BT as the key provider of domestic telephone lines and digital business lines, such as ISDN and, more recently, broadband (necessary if, for instance, you want to download films or music from the Internet in minutes rather than hours). However, BT is extremely successful in integrating telecommunications and IT technologies, and is already well established in the professional services sector with its consultancy subsidiary, Syntegra.

*Employment opportunities*

As you might expect from a huge organisation committed to employing high-calibre people, BT offers many exciting career prospects and is keen to promote and offer opportunities at all levels within the company.

To apply for the BT Modern Apprenticeship Scheme you will need to:

- be eligible to work in the UK;

- be aged between 16 and 21 on 1 September 2004 (or 16–24 for Northern Ireland);

- have – or expect to have – a minimum of three, four or five GCSEs at grade C or above (or equivalent) in English Language and maths (standard level one, two or three in Scotland);

- have grade C or above in physics, combined sciences, computing or IT;

- be a good communicator who enjoys helping people and solving problems;

- be diligent and punctual in your work and training.

Some vacancies require higher qualifications; BT also welcomes applications from those who have A-levels.

To join BT's graduate programme, you will need to have or be expected to receive a 2:1 honours degree, or better. You must also have GCSE maths and English language at grade C or above, or equivalent qualifications. With a degree in Computer Science or Information Technology, opportunities exist in many business areas – a few of the key ones are:

- sales technical specialist;

- research and development;

- Internet and multimedia applications;

- systems and software;

- project management.

Sandwich placements are available, as are student skills training workshops.

# MULTIMEDIA

The continuing rapid development of technology to present information in novel forms is creating vibrant, dynamic, multimedia enterprises. Most information can now be digitised: text, sound, image (still and moving) and touch are presented in exciting, innovative, artistic forms. Multimedia will increasingly embrace entertainment and education, as well as business, as the world becomes connected to the Internet. We can only surmise how careers will develop, but it will be an exciting area combining media knowledge with technical skills. Entry is possible through either media design or software experience, and creativity is important. Jobs and roles within this sector are further explored in Chapter 6.

The multimedia industry is predicted to be the key growth area over the next decade, such is the interest in the uses to which multimedia technology can be put. Entry into this area requires a good mix of creative and technical skills. Likely candidates will possess a good degree in media design, software engineering or an arts-related subject.

---

*FACT FILE*

In 1995 more than 100 Sun systems were used to produce images for Disney's *Toy Story* – the first computer-generated feature film.

---

# THE COMPUTER GAMES INDUSTRY

Computer game production is now the fastest growing segment of the entertainment industry, being double the size of the video rental market and nearly one-and-a-half times larger than cinema box office receipts. The UK gaming industry brought in £2 billion in 2003 and deserves to be taken as seriously as the domestic film industry.

Compared to the offerings from today's computer games industry, the early *Space Invaders* and *PacMan* arcade games now seem like child's play; they did, however, hook a generation of children and adults onto the concept of the computer game.

As this book was being written, SCI Entertainment, a producer of computer games, reported a pre-tax leap in profits to £3.5 million and turnover increased by 61 per cent to £28.5 million.

## Game console manufacturers

The Sony Corporation has a long and successful history in the entertainment business is a perfect example of how such changes can lead to great success! Following the huge success of its market-leading PlayStation and PS games consoles, shipments of these consoles are beginning to level off as new gaming strategies emerge.

New consoles, such as the PS3 and X-Box3 will ensure growth in gaming, as will the rise in gaming services available over the Internet. Additionally, the relatively new paid-for online games subscriptions concept is forecast to take over from 2004–05, around about the same time as the new consoles will be hitting the shelves. The prospects are encouraging, which means there will be many more opportunities in all IT areas connected with gaming in general.

## Games software companies

Mega-selling games are not the product of one company; they are the end product from a number of companies. This is no coincidence: a lot of specialist skills are needed for companies to bring to market a product that in many ways is the computer equivalent of a blockbuster Hollywood movie.

Companies such as Eidos (the company behind *Tomb Raider*) do not actually write computer games software, but provide an 'umbrella group' under which lie a number of smaller companies specialising in areas such as marketing, advertising, distribution and research. The actual design and programming aspects of the production of computer games are normally performed by a number of small, independent software development studios that are commissioned to supply computer games by the big umbrella companies.

# THE ELECTRONIC PUBLISHING INDUSTRY

The electronic publishing industry is rapidly emerging as one of the most successful sectors within the information technology profession. With the almost seamless transition from floppy disk to CD-ROM (compact disk, read only memory), and now to digital versatile disk (DVD), the products of this new 'multimedia' industry are readily used both in the home and within business.

Just 15 years ago, a typical magazine journalist would have relied upon shorthand notes and a typewriter to capture the latest news events, usually within the bounds of a district or city. Now, with the advances of IT, virtually every aspect of this industry has changed.

The biggest change has come, not surprisingly, as a result of the development of the Internet as a mature tool for business, providing publishing and news industries with access to global information as it happens, in real time.

Like many other 'new' industries that have emerged from the growth of the 'information society', electronic publishing has its roots firmly based in a very old industry – publishing. While the key objectives of the publishing industry have changed little, the way in which they are now achieved using IT is considerably different to the techniques used 10 years ago.

The multimedia industry is a big user of expensive PC-based hardware and software; and while publishing techniques have changed, the objectives are still the same: to make money by selling a quality product. To develop the product (newspapers, books, videos and so on), specialist IT hardware and software is often necessary so that the complex images required can be transposed onto a wide variety of media, such as paper, CD-ROM, DVD and, of course, the Web.

The scope for rewarding careers in this fast-moving, demanding industry is high. IT skills are used alongside publishing skills to provide many varied roles and responsibilities. Publishing tasks will involve writing, editing, proofreading and design work. IT tasks will involve supporting the hardware, software and networks; writing in-house software for publishing tasks or even producing encryption algorithms to protect information (such as electronic books and applications) distributed on CD-ROM.

The main software packages used in the electronic publishing industry fall into two categories: desktop publishing software and photo-imaging software. *Desktop publishing software* is similar to word-processing software, but is used for editing and controlling multiple documents, such as the sections of a newspaper or chapters in a book. One of the most popular desktop publishing packages used in the industry is QuarkXPress.

*Photo-imaging software.* Practically all of the images (ie pictures, photographs and diagrams) found in books and newspapers are now produced electronically, using digital image-editing programs and scanners. With these publishing tools, source images, such as photographs, can be 'scanned' into the computer and edited using specialist software. This software is similar to an art or graphics package that might be used in the home, allowing parts of the image to be edited. A good example of how this is used within the electronic publishing industry can be found on the front page of the 'glossy' fashion magazines: photographs of models (especially close-up facial shots) are often 'touched up' to appear perfect. One of the most popular imaging and graphics packages used in the industry is Adobe Photoshop.

## Qualifications required

The qualifications you need largely depend on the level at which you wish to enter the industry. A degree in maths, physics or IT (with a passing interest in art and design!) will allow you entry to the more senior levels. If, however, you prefer to enter the industry with 'real' skills rather than academic qualifications, you might want to consider courses offering vocational skills and training. Courses such as a GNVQ in Art and Design and Computing will provide you with the basic skills you need.

## PEARSON PUBLISHING

Pearson Publishing is a small group of businesses that produce high-quality educational products and services on various forms of electronic multimedia as well as on the traditional 'printed page'. In practice, this means the company not only produces materials on 'fixed' electronic media such as CD-ROM, but also on 'online' media, such as the Web.

Specialising in information and communications technology, the company's emphasis is on applying new technologies to the preparation of teaching, training and marketing materials.

### Career opportunities

Being one of the smaller companies in this sector (not to be confused with the huge international multimedia company, Pearson plc), it needs highly motivated and bright people who can quickly become experts in all the major areas of multimedia publishing. While publishing tasks such as design, editing and proofreading are performed, these form only a part of the whole operation. Specific IT tasks such as building networks, writing in-house software, building demonstrations and supporting all the IT hardware and software are also performed.

Most of its employees are graduates, who have studied maths, physics or computing. However, the company also employs students who possess A-levels, not necessarily in IT and computing, though this helps.

# Deciding where to work

**4**

Computing and IT is now used in practically every business organisation worldwide to perform many different functions. New entrants into the IT industry will therefore have a wide range of career opportunities available to them, such as working for the armed forces, undertaking scientific research or working within academia. However, the majority of school-leavers, students and graduates seeking a career in IT will be most likely to find employment either developing or supporting IT systems in the private or public sector. The aim of this chapter is to highlight some of the main business sectors where you are most likely to find employment as an IT user or practitioner.

## FINANCIAL SERVICES

The changes in our banking habits, such as the widespread use of the ATM, financial call centres and Internet banking are all a result of continued investment in IT by the banking and finance industries. By using the Internet to provide more cost-effective online banking and share-dealing services, this sector more than ever is now dependent on computing and IT. As an example, the cost of customers using a bank's Web site has been estimated at just 0.1 per cent of the cost of a transaction undertaken with a branch office.

## FACT FILE

Users spend $2 trillion on Visa cards each year, and 250,000 Web-based traders accept payment using the Internet.

When Halifax and Bank of Scotland merged to form HBOS in 2001, 4,000 IT staff worked on systems integration projects, reducing the number of conflicting and duplicated IT systems.

## BARCLAYS PLC

Barclays is one of the largest financial services groups in the UK. Within the Barclays group however, the company has banking and investment interests well beyond the UK. In terms of IT, Barclays is renowned for investing large sums in IT projects, from IT infrastructure and architecture to leading-edge software development and e-commerce. The IT and Operations business functional area is where company-wide IT strategy is formulated and implemented through one or more IT programmes.

*Graduate careers*

Graduates can join the Business Leadership Programme, which gives graduates high levels of exposure to many Barclays operations. The programme is structured around an accelerated development environment and a framework to help graduates succeed in their chosen career path.

Minimum degree qualifications are, ideally, a 2:1 degree in any discipline and 22 (280) UCAS points. However, Barclays will consider applicants with relevant work experience who do not meet these academic requirements but complete an excellent application.

Graduate starting salary is £23,000 plus £3,000 joining bonus and up to £3,550 mobility allowance.

*Application procedure*

Speculative applications are welcome. Barclays uses numerical psychometric tests to screen applicants and offers industrial placements in the form of an eight-week Summer Business Programme.

# THE PUBLIC SECTOR

The public sector is investing large sums of money in IT infrastructure and services. The present UK government has a mandate to improve many public services and is prepared to meet that challenge by investing in IT. For the newcomer to computing and IT, the public sector now offers good opportunities for career development up to the highest levels, both as an IT user and as an IT practitioner. Not only do public sector IT staff tend to stay longer in their jobs than their counterparts in private industry, they also feel they make a greater social contribution as well.

Contrary to popular belief that the public sector cannot offer a rewarding IT career, it might surprise you to know that the public sector in the UK runs some of the largest and most complex IT projects in Europe. The National Health Service alone is pioneering new technology all the time, allowing the sharing of medical records and clinical data in the quest for greater benefits.

## FACT FILE

With a £3.2 billion budget for the first three years, the National Programme for NHS IT is one of the most expensive projects in the public sector.

The NHS Web site (www.nhs.uk) provides the public with a single source of information about local health services and was recently voted public sector IT project of the year by *Computing* magazine. The site is searchable by postcode and includes maps and opening times for every GP, hospital, optician, dentist and pharmacy in England, as well as information on waiting times for all 26,000 consultants working in NHS Trusts.

# PROFESSIONAL SERVICES

Companies offering professional services provide consultancy and IT services that help organisations transform the way they operate by applying business knowledge and technological solutions. Activities include business consultancy, complex programme management and custom systems design, development and operation.

## SYNTEGRA

Syntegra is part of the BT group and has a graduate programme consisting of two distinct streams: Business Stream and Technology Stream. The former concentrates on working with business clients to define and develop IT solutions, the latter more on technology. Graduates on the Business Stream programme do not need to have an IT degree, but as the Technology Stream is technical in nature, this is essential.

*Graduate careers*

Ten per cent of Syntegra's graduates are from non-IT disciplines. Subjects of particular interest are: Business, Computing, Physics and Maths. The company will consider conversion-course graduates. The minimum degree qualification is 2.2. Typical graduate roles are:

business analyst, project management trainee, consultant, security consultant and sales. Graduate starting salary is £25,000 plus flexible benefits.

*Application procedure*

Speculative applications are welcome and the company uses diagrammatic reasoning as part of its psychometric testing of job applicants.

*Industrial placement programme*

Syntegra offers a one-year industrial placement to technical students wishing to expand their technical and business experience. During the 12 months there is the chance to work on multi-million pound customer projects and to get involved at various stages of the project life cycle, from development through to delivery and support.

# RETAIL

The UK's top 100 retailers, including Tesco, Sainsbury's, Asda and Safeway spent £1.8 billion on IT in 2003 – a rise of 27 per cent on the previous 12 months. Not only does this indicate that there is a growing realisation that information technology can be used effectively to deliver real business benefits, it also means that the retail sector can offer some of the best career opportunities for those seeking a career in IT.

Within this sector, a number of key technologies are now high on IT directors' priorities, such as 'chip and pin' (credit cards that require customers to enter a PIN to authenticate their transaction), using radio frequency identification (RFID) to improve the supply chain, mobile technologies and an increasing reliance on Internet technologies. However, the retail sector is not just at the forefront of new technology: commercial software development, which has often been less of a priority, is now increasing in importance.

# TESCO

Tesco is now the UK's largest private sector employer and, at the time of writing, is the largest e-grocer and the most profitable e-retail business in the world. To support Tesco's increasing customer base and retail operations there is expected to be a continued investment in IT.

## Graduate careers

There are good career opportunities for those seeking a career in IT. Tesco has a well-established graduate programme, which incorporates both business and technical training, store placements and an IT functional area. On completion of the programme, graduates will join one of the following IT teams:

- service delivery – focused on providing support to internal customers through business systems development;

- technology and architecture – focus on technology, designing new systems to support Tesco's future needs in a global marketplace;

- strategic development – key systems development, building systems to meet the requirements of Tesco's headlining business projects.

## Applications

The company expects candidates to possess excellent problem-solving skills, a keen interest in technology and commercial awareness. It will consider conversion-course graduates and expects a minimum degree qualifications of 2:1 in any discipline. Typical graduate roles are systems analyst and systems developer.

# AIRLINE TRAVEL

Reservation systems, ticketing systems and in-flight services are just a few of the types of business applications used within the travel industry. They all require huge computer systems and databases to store customer and flight information from travel agencies and airline companies situated all over the world. In the early 1980s, global distribution systems were used by airlines to sell tickets (in many ways, like the Internet), giving access to airline fares to travel agents across the world.

Before the 'boom and bust' of the Internet during the late 1990s, Internet technology had already transformed the travel industry. Online selling has expanded the travel market while bringing lower fares to passengers. With the technology supporting the travel sector advancing all the time, it won't be long before all the travel options available to the customer, such as seat reservation, booking amendment, meal choice, check-in and car hire will be performed using Web services.

## *BRITISH AIRWAYS*

Within British Airways (BA), IT drives everything: reservations, passenger check-in, flight planning, communications networks, supply chain and inventory to name but a few. Some of this technology, as you might expect, is leading edge; some of it is quite a few years' old. Age, however, is not important in the IT industry when it comes to software: it's what you do with it that matters.

*Career opportunities*

BA is a heavily reliant upon IT and its use of IT is widespread: sales and reservations services; electronic ticketing initiatives; systems that plan the optimum use of fuel; and even devising the latest in-flight entertainment. Without computing and IT, BA would not be able to operate; its remit covers everything from development and support of computing systems for its customers, staff and business partners worldwide. In every sense of the word, BA is a big player within the airline travel sector; its £350 million business is among the top 10 IT departments in the UK.

The IT function within BA is split into two broad areas: IT strategy and IT delivery – an overview of each area is shown in Table 4.1.

**Table 4.1** The role of the BA IT strategy and delivery teams

| IT strategy team | *Business solutions.* Works with the airline to identify how IT can best support business change, and shape the required IT projects so that they are suitable for delivery. |
| --- | --- |
| | *Technical solutions.* Design and maintain the IT standards necessary to support the IT infrastructure. |
| | *e-Business innovation.* Promote innovative change across BA through the use of e-commerce technologies and e-working initiatives. |
| | *Architecture team.* Responsible for ensuring that BA has a coherent design across all its IT systems – whether they have been developed within BA or not. |
| IT delivery team | *Applications delivery.* Responsible for building and integrating IT solutions, delivering the software that is used throughout BA to run its business. |
| | *Resource management.* Aim to provide high-quality, skilled people to deliver the IT solutions that the BA business demands. |
| | *Service delivery.* Implement, operate and maintain the end-to-end IT environment BA needs to deliver its products and services and to manage its internal business. The airline business works 24 hours a day, 365 days a year. |
| | *Infrastructure delivery.* Provide timely, cost-effective delivery of the airline's IT infrastructure, spanning mainframe and mid-range computers, PCs and voice and data networks. |

## Graduate entry

BA operates an IT Professionals Scheme for new graduates. Graduates joining the scheme tend to specialise in two main areas. The first is as part of the operations function, looking at the technical aspects of the equipment and operating software that supply the infrastructure and keep BA's systems running. This demands everything from advanced technical skills to the ability to become involved in complex business issues such as licensing, resourcing and planning for disaster recovery. There are also legacy responsibilities, as well as maintenance and programming tasks.

The second area is the development and maintenance of applications that are key in giving BA an advantage over its competitors, and enables it to find more efficient ways of conducting its business. This role involves programming/development within any of its current applications.

### Applications

The company will consider conversion-course graduates and candidates without an IT degree; however, the latter are expected to show an interest in IT. Minimum qualifications are: a degree (see Web site for specific details); the right to live and work in the UK; GCSEs in maths and English at grade C or above (or equivalent); and a keen interest and aptitude for IT. Typical graduate roles are: applications development, business analysis and systems management.

### Application procedure

Speculative applications are welcome and psychometric tests are used to assess applicants.

### FACT FILE

Research by BA found that 75 per cent of its business travellers fly with laptops and want Internet access.

# PHARMACEUTICALS

Today's pharmaceuticals industry would not survive without the advances in IT and computing technology achieved over the past decade. The pharmaceuticals sector is like any other commercial sector in the sense that it is dominated by a few large multinationals, but in some ways it is unique among IT users, with relatively small, recently created companies employing only a few hundred people, but using more computer power than many multinational organisations.

## GLAXOSMITHKLINE

Formed from the merger of two huge pharmaceuticals companies, SmithKlineBeecham and Glaxo, GSK in now the largest pharmaceuticals company in Europe, with a world-leading research operation.

*Graduate careers*

IT within GSK is split into a number of different units that work closely with the business to meet the specific needs of that business function. For instance, Global Manufacturing and Supply IT and R&D IT deliver the IT component of business improvement projects.

Addressing the core needs of the various business units and projects are teams such as Systems and Communications Services, who manage the IT infrastructure, and Global IT Risk Management, who address IT risks that present a potential threat to GSK.

*Graduate programme structure*

GSK has an excellent graduate programme to help its graduates (known as Associates) develop their IT skills through accelerated learning and support. The IT development programme runs for three years and provides a structured, high-quality, broad-based approach to the training and development of new graduates. While on the programme, Associates are supported by a Sponsors Group, a Management Operations Committee, a programme manager, their current line manager, a mentor and a buddy. Continued networking opportunities are supported through Graduate Forums and informal social activities.

### Training and development

Training and development is undertaken to ensure the continued development of Associates in a flexible manner that meets the needs of both the individual and the business. While on the IT Development Programme, 20 per cent of an Associate's working week is allocated to professional development. This may take the form of day release to university, study leave or exam leave.

### Applications

The company will consider conversion-course graduates and does not stipulate a minimum degree qualification. Typical graduate roles are scientists. GSK does not welcome speculative applications and details of the application procedure can be found by contacting the GSK Response Centre (see Chapter 9 for contact details). Logic reasoning psychometric tests are used to assess applicants.

# EDUCATION

With the focus often placed on business and commerce, it is easy to forget the crucial role IT plays within the academic world. Whether you decide to become a school teacher or a university researcher, you will be faced with as many challenges – in many ways more challenges – than people working in business. Information and Communications Technology (ICT) is taught as part of the National Curriculum from primary school upwards, and is in fact the only fundamentally *new* subject in the National Curriculum. (Table 4.2 provides details of where you can teach ICT.) In further and higher education, more and more computing-related subjects are being introduced to meet the demands of business and commerce as well as for future research activity.

**Table 4.2**  Opportunities for teaching ICT

| Secondary schools | ✓ |
|---|---|
| City Technology Colleges (CTCs) | ✓ |
| Further education (FE) colleges | ✓ |
| Sixth-form colleges | ✓ |
| Universities | ✓ |

ICT *is* taught in primary education, but to teach at this level, you will first need to learn specialised teaching methods and be able to teach in a wide range of other subjects as well as information technology.

## Working in secondary education

If you want to teach ICT in a state-maintained secondary school you must first become a qualified teacher. This can be achieved in a number of different ways, but they will all provide you with, at a minimum, Qualified Teacher Status (QTS).

In most cases, QTS is achieved by following an approved course of Initial Teacher Training (ITT). Before you start your ITT course, you must have already gained the equivalent of GCSE grade C (or above) in both English language and mathematics. The two main routes to obtain QTS are by completing a degree course or a postgraduate course. These courses are run in schools, colleges and universities throughout the UK.

Additionally, secondary teachers need subject knowledge at degree level in the subject(s) they are trained to teach. To teach ICT on an undergraduate ITT programme, this subject knowledge will be studied as part of your degree.

## Degree courses for teacher training

Any one of the following degrees will enable you to enter the teaching profession while also providing you with a professional qualification. They are all usually four years in length, combining a standard degree with a year of teacher training:

▓ BEd (Bachelor of Education) a shortened two-year course is also available;

▓ BA (Bachelor of Arts) with QTS;

▓ BSc (Bachelor of Science) with QTS.

*Minimum entry requirements*

Five different subjects (grade C or above) at GCSE level or equivalent, including English language and mathematics, are required. Two of these must be at A level or equivalent, such as BTEC National Award or GNVQ (General National Vocational Qualification) in computing or IT.

*Postgraduate courses for teacher training*

For secondary school teaching, the main route is by gaining a PGCE (Postgraduate Certificate in Education) after you have obtained a degree through the normal routes (your degree, however, must contain a strong element of computing or IT). The standard PGCE is a one-year full-time course that you can start either immediately after gaining your degree or return to after a number of years' work experience.

If you are a postgraduate on a PGCE leading to Qualified Teacher Status (QTS), you will receive a £6,000 bursary while on Initial Teacher Training as long as your Local Education Authority (LEA) is paying your tuition fees. As ICT is a priority subject within maintained schools and non-maintained special schools in England, you may be eligible for a £4,000 taxable 'golden hello'.

Typically, PGCE providers are universities or colleges of higher education, the Open University, and School or City Technology Colleges (School-Centred ITT).

## Open University PGCE courses

The Open University (OU) now runs distance-learning PGCE courses for secondary courses in IT subjects. These usually take 18 months to complete, combining periods of teaching practice and on-site school projects, making them comparable with a standard PGCE.

## Fast Track Programme

The Fast Track Programme (FTP) was launched in 2000 as a way of modernising the teaching profession. FTP is aimed at attracting the brightest and most ambitious graduates (and career changers) into the profession and so inspire others around them to achieve greater things. For students wanting to teach computing and information technology within secondary schools, ICT is a subject that you can study within the FTP.

## Alternative graduate entry

If you are 24 years or older, you can choose to take an employment-based route into teaching where you will earn while you train. On the Graduate Teacher Programme (GTP) and Registered Teacher Programme (RTP) you will receive a salary at least equivalent to the unqualified teacher pay rate (£13,266). The individual school may pay you more. The GTP is very popular and places are limited.

## Secondary Subject Shortage Scheme

If you are enrolled on an ITT programme in England covering ICT, you may be eligible for financial assistance under the Secondary Subject Shortage Scheme. This is a hardship fund and your college or university will assess whether you are eligible. If you are under 25, you will receive up to £5,000, and those who are 25 or older will receive up to £7,500.

Newly Qualified Teachers (NQT) who took out loans from the Student Loans Company may also be able to benefit from the Repayment of Teachers' Loans (RTL) scheme. If you teach ICT, your outstanding loan will be repaid by the government over a period of 10 years as long as you stay in teaching. To benefit from the RTL scheme, you should go straight into teaching after training and you must teach one or more of the priority subjects for at least half of your teaching time.

NQTs can expect to start at £18,139 per year, or £21,522 in Inner London. Advanced Skills Teachers concentrate on classroom work and developing the profession; they are paid between £26,082 and £41,607.

## Working in a college or university

Teachers who work in further and higher education are normally referred to as 'lecturers' and are paid on a slightly different pay scale to teachers. While you do not normally require a teaching qualification to become a college or university lecturer, you will almost certainly need a degree. A computing degree is preferred, but many other degrees are acceptable nowadays if they contain a substantial amount of IT. If you decide to train for a teaching post in further education, you may be eligible to have your student loan repaid under the Repayment of Teachers' Loans scheme.

There is one main difference between working in a college and in a university, and that is the emphasis placed upon research. With public sector funding constantly under threat, universities need to establish close links with industry in order to obtain funding for new research programmes and new staff. As a result, many universities are now more interested in the research opportunities potential lecturers can bring to the university (and therefore, what private funding they might attract) than their specific teaching skills. Competition is fierce for these positions, and if you *do* want to become a university lecturer, you will ideally be able to offer:

▓ a good honours degree in an IT subject (preferably a 2:1 or a first);

▓ a higher degree (MSc, MPhil, PhD, etc);

▓ specific research interests that match the university's own research programme.

Salaries for lecturers in colleges and universities can vary enormously, depending on the institution, funding levels and local demand. Starting salaries for a graduate can be as low as £15,000, but if you already possess industrial or research experience or have a higher degree, salaries tend to start at around £21,000. More senior lecturing positions attract salaries of around £35,000.

## Funded research

Do not be misled into thinking that the only way to achieve success in the IT profession is through the high-profile world of commercial computing, where salaries and benefit packages can seem irresistible.

Research is an exciting place for the IT professional, providing many opportunities to use and develop computer systems, often with state-of-the-art systems that would rarely be seen in the commercial sector. With investment returning to the IT world after some bleak periods, the opportunities for research have never been greater. Research projects currently attracting funding include:

- grid computing;
- Web services;
- computer security;
- biometric systems.

## Salaried research

If you want to join a university research project (usually funded by one of the European agencies), you should apply for a post as a research assistant, which carries a salary (vacancies will be advertised in the *Times Educational Supplement*). This post will normally be for a fixed-length term and you will need a very good computing degree and possibly even a higher degree as well (such as an MSc or PhD). Although research assistants often work unsupervised, they will usually report to a research director during the project, especially if it is funded externally. Typical salaries for a research assistant are between £14,000 and £20,000.

# Katie is a lecturer in Computer Science

After joining the IT industry as a computing graduate with an MSc in Computer Science and Artificial Intelligence, I soon realised that I was not using and developing my interpersonal skills as much as I would have liked. I've always enjoyed talking about IT issues as much as I have enjoyed the technical side of things, so it was only a matter of time before I started to look for a job in the teaching profession (although I knew very little about it at the time). If I had one worry, it was that I might end up becoming something out of 'Grange Hill' – losing all my computing skills but being a dab hand with the blackboard!

Finding a suitable job was relatively easy: vacancies for college lecturers appear in the *Times Educational Supplement* every week. However, while industry experience is useful within education, so too is teaching experience. To help bridge the gap I decided to try and teach part time first of all, by becoming an associate lecturer at a university nearby. This benefits both parties: I needed the experience of working as a lecturer and the university is always short of lecturers who are prepared to teach evening classes. Admittedly, I started off by only teaching basic and advanced courses in Microsoft Excel and Access, but it got me on the right career path. Shortly after, the university sent me on a City & Guilds course to learn the basics of teaching in higher education, which gave me even more confidence. Now, having applied for and gained a position as a full-time lecturer, I have a wide and varied programme of courses to teach, ranging from short modules on artificial intelligence to degree-level Systems Analysis and Design. Funding is a problem though, so I still have to teach one evening class a week at the moment.

Of course, I also have non-teaching responsibilities. I provide a 'pastoral' role for my students, and I do make time for them should they wish to discuss their problems with me, whatever they are – a responsibility which I take very seriously.

call into systems programmers, network administrators or database administrators.

## Main tasks

- Taking system backups onto computer tape.

- Scheduling daily, weekly and monthly work on the computer, eg monthly payroll applications.

- Loading computer tapes into tape drives for processing.

- Ensuring user applications have been started and stopped at the correct times.

- Producing statistics on the performance of the computer.

- Identifying and resolving computer system errors.

- Providing general support for the computer system and the applications running on it.

It is possible that in some organisations technical support is required for the IT systems outside normal business hours. In practice, this may be an informal agreement to 'man the phones' or it may be more formal, such as participating in a rota system and forming part of a contract of employment. If there is a need to work extended or unsociable hours, this should attract an increase in salary.

## Salary

Junior technical support analyst: £15,000 upwards. Senior technical support analyst: £30,000–40,000.

### Lee is a technical support analyst

Since graduating in IT, I have been working for an airline company, joining their Systems Management Team. The company has a multitude of IT systems to support the operation of the business, and it is my team that monitors these systems, regardless of whether they are UNIX, NT or mainframe systems. Automation tools allow us to reduce the amount of time we spend in the mainframe area by responding to messages, thus releasing us to do more important work.

The support we provide is critical to the operation of the airline and so we have to provide support 24 hours a day. This is performed on a rota basis by a separate team, which we have the option of joining for periods of time.

We also use a number of popular system-management tools, such as BMC Patrol, to help monitor our UNIX and NT servers (there are well over 300!), allowing us to deal with any potential problems before they impact on the business. More recently, I was sent on a training course to learn about computer security (especially on the Internet), as we are now moving towards e-commerce as a means of trading and the need for a secure and reliable service has never been more important.

# HELP-DESK ANALYST

The help desk is the area within the IT department that provides general help and advice to all the users of the computer system. Working with users who are experiencing problems with their IT hardware or software, the help desk analyst provides the first (and most important) point of contact between the IT department and the business departments within the organisation.

## Main tasks

While some help-desk analysts are highly skilled computer technicians, often resolving lengthy and complex user problems, the average help-desk operator would perform the following tasks:

- recording user problems;
- resolving day-to-day problems, such as users forgetting their system password;

- informing users of any maintenance work taking place on the computer system, which might prevent them from using it;

- passing more complex problems to the support teams for fixing;

- contacting computer manufacturers and suppliers if an error in one of their products is identified.

## Skills required

- Patience and understanding (not everyone is computer-literate!).

- Pleasing manner (by the time many users have contacted the help desk, they will have gone mad trying to get their system to work and they will probably take it out on you!).

- A general understanding of how computer systems work (many 'users' are confident in talking about how their PC is configured and how their applications work – are you?).

## Salary

Help-desk analyst: £15,000–18,000.

# PROJECT MANAGER

Most common IT development work is team based and it is the role of the project manager to ensure that the development team complete their tasks to the satisfaction of the customer, within the specified time and budget. An IT project could be an internal piece of work within an organisation or it could be external to the company, working for another organisation or IT software house.

## Skills required

A typical project manager does not need technical skills, although having a good understanding of IT concepts and issues is a benefit. Throughout the duration of the project, the project manager will coordinate and control the combined efforts of the project team. As a typical project team consists of systems analysts, programmers, testers, trainers and implementers, it is important that the project manager has a good awareness of the software development lifecycle.

Project managers must also have good communication skills as they deal with people all the time – either their own IT project team or the customer. A good project manager will listen to, understand and motivate the project team and liase effectively with the customer to ensure that they are happy. A project manager is an unusual breed of person: tough when required, yet flexible and accommodating when the need arises. Diplomacy and tact are as important in this job as hard-edged business acumen.

Traditionally, many project managers have come from either an IT development or analysis background or have commercial and business project management experience. Such is the demand for project managers, many of the larger IT consultancy companies now train IT graduates for project management roles working on client sites. While project managers do not necessarily need a degree in an IT-related subject, most are expected to have been on an accredited project management training course, such as those run by the Information Systems Examination Board (ISEB) or the Cranfield School of Management.

## Salary

Graduate project managers: £22,000–25,000. Experienced project managers: £25,000–50,000. Experienced freelance project managers: anything from £1,000 per week upwards.

### Anne is a project manager working for a consultancy company

Although I did gain a degree in computer science at Manchester University, I've never really considered myself to be technical. I've always been interested in the interaction between technology and people – which is why I think I've been quite successful as a project manager.

A technical author needs a rare set of skills, combining the roles of author and publisher with those of an IT specialist. While word-processing packages are widely used within the IT industry, a technical author will often use more sophisticated document-composition software, similar to the packages used within the electronic publishing industry. Starting salaries tend to fall in the range £12,000–15,000.

# TECHNICAL SUPPORT

## Systems programmer

Within all computer systems there are a number of programs and utilities that are used by the computer system itself; collectively they are called 'systems software'. Writing, installing and maintaining this software are the main tasks performed by the systems programmer.

Systems programmers will often have to manipulate special files or execute complex commands as part of their work. As these affect the computer system, there is always a risk of something going wrong, causing a major problem, which is why some of these tasks are performed at weekends when the computer system is not required by the users.

*Main tasks*

- Installing new versions of computer software (applications and operating systems).

- Fixing system-level errors on the computer.

- Configuring systems software, eg data back-up utilities.

- Tuning the computer system.

- Controlling access and security to the computer system.

- Providing second-line support when required.

*Salary*

Trainee systems programmers: £15,000–18,000. Graduate systems programmers: £22,000–25,000.

## Dave is a UNIX systems programmer

I graduated from Sheffield Hallam University with a degree in Computer Studies with one slight problem – I didn't really know what particular field of computing I wanted to move into. For many graduates, the standard entry points are programming or systems analysis; but to be honest, neither option inspired me! However, I did have a niggling urge to work at a more technical level within the profession, using hardware and software and really understanding how things worked. During my sandwich year with Fujitsu (what used to be known as ICL), I built and tested lots of hardware and software products as part of a UNIX system install procedure. I remembered how interesting this was when I graduated, but didn't know what sorts of jobs I should apply for to continue my interest. After speaking with the university careers staff, they suggested I apply for positions as a graduate systems programmer.

Not soon after, I joined a large retail organisation as a systems programmer in its computer support team. The UNIX and C skills I gained while at Sheffield proved very useful to begin with – even a basic knowledge is enough in the early days of being a systems programmer!

Luckily, I was able to pick up lots more technical skills from the team, and I was also sent on quite a few externally run technical courses to learn how to use the software tools needed to perform system backups and fault diagnosis.

### Database administrator

Many business applications access large amounts of information that are stored in a database. While there are many different types of databases available today, relational databases, such as Microsoft Access and Oracle, are probably the most popular. When information held in the database is added, updated or deleted by a user, it is called 'a transaction'. As you can imagine, over time, as more users run transactions against the database, it will gradually increase in size and, if left unmanaged, will eventually cause problems. It is vitally important that the structure of the database and the complex relationships between the data are maintained regularly by the database administrator, otherwise inconsistencies could arise.

## Main tasks

■ Maintaining the integrity of the data within the database (is the data stored within it valid and accurate?).

■ Ensuring the database can be recovered in the event of an error (eg computer crash, virus or power failure).

■ Tuning the database (will the database still perform well when more data are added to it?).

■ Sizing the database (how large will it need to be in the future?).

## Salary

Trainee database administrators: £13,000–16,000. Graduate database administrators: £18,000–20,000.

## Gary is a database administrator

When I was at school all those years ago, I was not very academic and did not really think I could get a degree – in any subject! However, my passion was computers and I was persuaded to enrol for an HND in Computing at my local college. HNDs are different from a typical degree as they are more relevant to the actual skills you will need within the IT industry, as opposed to learning the science of computing. When I left college I was raring to go and applied for a position as a trainee technical support specialist within Asda. To be honest, I didn't realise how much computing power supermarkets needed – their systems were huge (not in size, but power) and they used all the latest technologies to ensure that their retail operations were performed effectively.

Eventually I became a technical team leader, and while I was happy supporting the various computer systems within the company, I decided I wanted to specialise within the team and help support the many databases that existed on our UNIX systems. To help make the transition, I was sent on an Oracle 9 for administrators course in London to learn how to install and configure the Oracle database, which lasted a week. In addition, on the last day of the course, I sat an exam to become a certified Oracle database administrator, which I passed.

A few months later, I was promoted to Database Administrator within the team. To be honest, things were hectic at first and I ended up working quite a few weekends to tune the database parameters as it was the only time I could get to close the database down without affecting the users. I'm glad to say the system is working fine now, requiring very little maintenance, which has allowed me time to get involved with the next database project!

## Hardware support engineer

Many new servers are custom-built to user requirements, and it will be a hardware engineer who captures the technical specifications for the server, builds it and then tests the system. While a hardware engineer will perform many routine tasks, such as plugging together and integrating a number of separate hardware components, many more tasks will be highly complex and the challenge facing hardware engineers is to keep abreast of the latest technologies. Obviously, for this sort of role an interest in electronics is useful as well as a good understanding of computer technology. Typically, a degree is required for senior engineer roles, but many companies will take on school-leavers with GCSEs and provide training.

*Main tasks*

▨ Replacing or repairing faulty computer equipment.

▨ Performing diagnostics on devices suspected of being faulty, usually by running diagnostic computer software that identifies faults and recommends solutions.

*Skills required*

▨ Degree in Computer Science.

▨ Knowledge of computing hardware, including PC builds.

▨ Specific hardware vendor skills and accreditation are desirable, such as those available from IBM, HP and Sun Microsystems.

*Salary*
Hardware support engineer: £15,000 – 18,000.

# NETWORKING SERVICES

## Network administrator

A network administrator will often work closely with telecommunications companies and networking hardware suppliers to build local area networks (LANs) and wide area network (WANs). A LAN will typically connect a number of computers within a department or building, whereas a WAN will connect computers to different sites across the country, using public or private telephone lines.

As you can imagine, with hundreds or even thousands of users connected over a network, the scope for error is quite high. Network administrators will help the network designers in building a network, but their main function will be to manage and support the network once it has been built – identifying and resolving faults is a key task for a network administrator!

*Main tasks*

▨ Connecting computers to LANs and WANs, on mainframe, mid-range or desktop platforms.

- Designing and building networks using technologies such as Ethernet and Token Ring.

- Configuring network software to add new connections or restrict access to certain users on the network (authentication).

- Identifying and resolving errors on the network, such as data congestion and slow response times.

- Ensuring the network is protected against computer viruses and hackers, for example by building a 'firewall' or installing anti-virus software.

### Skills required

- Knowledge of networking software and communication protocols, such as TCP/IP (Transmission Control Protocol/ Internet Protocol – a networking protocol popular in UNIX networks and on the Internet).

- Knowledge of networking hardware, such as network cards, token ring adapters and hubs.

- A basic knowledge of Internet and network security.

### Salary

Network administrator: £12,000–15,000. Graduates with network administration experience: £18,000–20,000.

## Mike is a network administrator responsible for a number of departmental LANs

Having spent three years working for a large airline as a graduate support technician, I was never really interested in networking at first. Like most of my colleagues, I did not really appreciate networking, and I suppose I just saw it as messing around with lots of cables and switches.

My opinion soon changed when the company expanded its mainframe computer system to incorporate

UNIX and NT systems. All of a sudden, the network became something we could all associate with, as we all started having Ethernet cards slotted in our PCs and we were all given IP addresses showing our unique address on the network. I realised that working in the network team could be an exciting move for me, and I haven't looked back since. The company sent me on a few basic courses to learn about the major protocols used on the network – TCP/IP and SNMP – and within a few weeks the whole fuzzy area of networking became clear! The networking team are now investigating Internet security, as, like most other companies, we are all aware of the threats posed by malicious hackers, computer viruses and IT system security in general. The company has already sent me on a basic course to understand about security and e-security (specific to Internet-based activities) and I'm hoping one day to specialise in computer security.

## Network designer

This area is for those who wish to work with clients to help them formulate, then specify and design their communications needs into viable networks. Communications network designers need to understand current and emerging technologies and how they can be exploited to satisfy client needs, from wiring up a single site, to a worldwide network supported by different technologies. The role demands that designers know enough about business needs to be able to assist clients to create their communications requirements, then derive technical solutions. Network design is fiercely competitive and fast developing, with client expectations rising all the time; this is a career for those who relish working with clients to develop technological solutions in a challenging commercial environment. Entry usually requires some technical communications experience or a relevant degree.

## Andrew is a network designer

While studying for my degree (in Geography), I became interested in communications technology – yes I know it sounds unlikely, but I suspect my trying to understand the basics of IP (Internet Protocol) and the Internet had something to do with it.

After graduating, I continued my studies and earned an MSc in Communication Systems. As part of my postgraduate degree, I managed to find a research project placement at BT Labs, where I became involved in the principle and operation of high-speed broadband networking.

I later joined another telecommunications company as a network designer. My job is both challenging and rewarding, with lots of opportunities for career development. Oddly enough, while my role is technical, I have to work with and communicate with many other people, typically customers, colleagues and suppliers of equipment, in some cases, from countries outside the UK – which I like as it means I get to travel abroad on small assignments!

# FREELANCE IT CONTRACTORS

Flexibility is the key to working as a freelance contractor. If you are willing to work anywhere, on any project, you can expect to be rewarded well for your efforts. Most contractors work for themselves in the sense that they own their own company, into which their salary is paid by the organisation for which they are working. While the idea of being the managing director of your own company may boost your ego, it does have its drawbacks. For one thing, you will have to pay National Insurance Contributions both as an employee *and* an employer. You will also have to pay for any training you require (unless you can make 'an arrangement' with the organisation you are working with) and lose your entitlement to company sick pay.

Contractors are required in all the major areas of IT support and development for all sorts of reasons – the main one being to meet a short-term skills requirement on a major project. For this reason, most contracts are between three and six months' long, but contracts of 12 months are now becoming more common as well. Hundreds of jobs for contractors are advertised every week in *Computing* and *Computer Weekly*, but there are a number of IT magazines specifically aimed for those working as contractors, such as *Freelance Informer* and *Computer Contractor*.

## Income

On average, a freelance IT contractor can expect to earn £1,000 a week. Well-paid contracts for skills in demand can attract £2,000 a week.

# 6

# Jobs in multimedia, sales and training

The aim of this chapter is to give you a brief understanding of some of the jobs and roles that are not usually performed within a commercial IT department. They are still IT-related jobs of course, but they are not concerned with developing or supporting commercial business systems. As in the previous chapter, the case studies included here have been written by IT professionals who actually perform the roles discussed. You can treat what they say as a first-hand, accurate account of how they entered the IT industry and how their careers have developed within it.

## COMPUTER GAME DEVELOPMENT

The structure of a typical computer game development studio is shown in Figure 6.1.

### Software games developer

Software games developers working for games companies develop games software from an initial idea or design. There will often be more than one programmer working in a team, with each programmer working on a separate piece of the game. Games programmers today have the benefit of being able to use sophisticated computer packages, but programming skills are still extremely important.

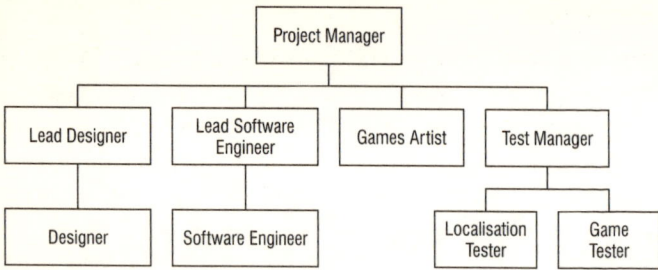

**Figure 6.1** The structure of a typical computer game development studio

## Skills required

Despite what you might think, this is not a job for amateur programmers who like playing computer games. Modern games programming has a high mathematical emphasis and requires a disciplined approach to programming. Even if you have taught yourself how to write computer programs from a tutorial program, this does not mean you possess the right 'professional' skills to work as a programmer, such as teamworking and problem-solving. For this reason, most companies will expect you to possess a good degree (2:1 or first class) from a respected university. The degree should be in one of the following subjects: computing, software engineering, mathematics, physics or engineering.

There are 'junior' positions available, where a degree is not always necessary, but do not hold out too much hope if you only have GCSEs or A levels. If you do not have a degree, you must be able to demonstrate that you are an *exceptionally* good programmer who can write structured and easily maintainable code. Most games companies will want to review a sample game or routine you have written to prove your programming competence.

A good working knowledge of programming languages used for gaming, such as C, C++ and Assembler is needed if you want to be a games programmer. In addition, a knowledge of artificial intelligence (AI) techniques and 3D programming and animation techniques, such as 3D Studio MAX, would be useful.

## Games artist

A computer games artist is responsible for creating the images used within a computer game, such as characters, scenery and on-screen instructions. If the game uses complex moving images, specialist graphics packages such as 3D Studio MAX will be used, which will save a lot of time and effort (and consequently cost).

*Skills required*

As you might expect, to be a games artist, you will need to be a good artist rather than an IT expert. Games software companies can teach artists relevant computer skills, but they can't teach an IT expert how to be a good artist!

## Games designer

A games designer performs a number of roles, depending on the size of the development studio. If the studio employs just a few people, the games designer may well be involved in everything from designing the game (plot, characters and scenery), writing manuals and in-game text, to planning how the special visual effects and music editing tasks need to be incorporated into the game. The designer will often work closely with the project manager from the initial concept to the finished computer game.

*Skills required*

A games designer performs a crucial role in the development of a computer game and it is not an area you would move into without previous experience of the games industry. In practice, a games designer will need a number of skills such as design, project management, scheduling and research. To help in this role, many designers use specialist computer packages that are written by the development studio, as opposed to buying an 'off-the-shelf' package.

## Games tester

The games tester plays an important (and enviable) role in the development of a computer game. Testing must be methodical and thorough to ensure that the game has been written to the design specification, incorporating any short cuts, tricks and bonus screens that may have been included in the game. While casual playing of the game may detect the obvious errors, only many hours of testing every option and route within the game will uncover the smaller errors, which if not picked up before distribution will cause many problems.

*Skills required*
PC and game-playing skills are essential, but good planning skills and a methodical approach to work are equally important. To be able to test a game, the tester must first understand how the game *should* work; for instance, what should the screens look like? How should the controls operate? How well is the music synchronised to events within the game? The ability to grasp and manage complex interdependent tasks quickly is vital in this role.

## Localisation tester

Before games written for the UK market can be sold in other countries, changes may need to be made to the screen displays or the instruction manual. It is the role of the localisation tester to test such games during their transition from the original English into the localised version that will be used in the country of purchase. The localisation tester will ensure all translations made are correct and proofread all the manuals.

*Skills required*
Fluency in foreign languages (mainly European) is essential, as is a high degree of competence in the English language. A good understanding of PCs is important – and you must enjoy playing computer games!

## What will the work be like?

A career in the computer games industry will involve working in a highly competitive market with many commercial pressures (just think of the Christmas games sales every year). With so many excellent games companies operating within the sector, often the only difference between success and failure is how quickly they can get their game into the shops.

More often than not you will be working in a team throughout the life cycle of the product, from designing the original game to completing the finished version ready for sale. During the early stages of development, the average team size is small (around six people), but towards the end of the project, when pressure to get the game completed and marketed is greater, the team will reach nearer 30 in number. Throughout the project you will often need to communicate with non-IT people, such as artists and sound engineers, so communication and planning skills will be important. These skills are taught on degree courses, which is another reason why there is a demand for high-calibre graduates in this industry.

## Salary

The average entry-level salary is around £17,000–19,000 for all positions, rising to over £40,000. In addition, you can expect to earn royalties based on sales.

## Further information

A useful source of information for anyone interested in this area would be any one of the many magazines specialising in computer games. *The Edge* is a particularly good source of information, providing details on the products, companies and career opportunities within the industry, and is read by many existing games designers and programmers.

Specific information on particular game companies and development studios can usually be found on their own Web sites (again, have a look in *The Edge* for company information).

### Chris is a junior games programmer

I left school at 16 with GCSEs and no definite career plans, although I was quite interested in computers. As luck would have it, I saw an advert for a government-sponsored IT training scheme and joined the same day.

As part of the training scheme, I started work in a local computer shop selling microcomputers and computer peripherals. Although I enjoyed meeting people and talking about computers, software and accessories, I preferred working in the offices, where I was allowed to help fix some of the computers. Luckily, as I showed an interest in the more fundamental aspects of computers, I was allowed to help write some of their own games software. At this stage, it was nothing too complicated, mainly just understanding how the game was written and the routines used to load the software onto the microcomputer. I was still keen, so they taught me assembler language, which is what most of the games programs and utilities were written in.

A few years later, after seeing an advert on TV for a games software company needing new games programmers, I applied. I had to write a small game to be reviewed by the company as well as attend an interview. I got the job and haven't looked back. I'm a much better programmer now, and I'm also proficient in C too, which means I'm very much more marketable when I decide to move on!

## IT SALES

In some ways, being in computer sales is one of the most important roles within the IT profession, and it is probably one of the best paid too. IT sales staff provide businesses with the computer hardware, software and services they need to solve their problems and increase profitability. While sales staff have an understanding of computer systems, they will often rely on IT specialists to help them during the sales process, both before and after the sale (bid management, pre-sales support and post-sales support). A good knowledge of business, often in a specific field such as retail or personnel systems is essential, as is a shrewd mind for figures. Salaries for sales staff are usually high, with part of their salary usually in the form of a commission, based on the value of the sales. Many top sales staff are graduates, who can combine their technical expertise with management skills they have developed. However, there are opportunities for people from many diverse backgrounds to move into sales, maybe after performing a marketing or pre-sales support role.

## Salary

Salaries in sales can vary enormously depending on the amount of commission received. An average base salary (excluding commission) could be anywhere between £30,000 and £60,000, but six-figure salaries are achievable in many of the larger IT companies.

### Angela works within the sales function for an IT hardware and software vendor

Although I'm in sales, my official job title is 'Account Manager' – its a bit more customer friendly than 'salesman' (or 'saleswoman')! Working for a large software house whose products are written for all the popular operating systems, I don't really need to 'sell' products as such – IT managers or procurement managers tend to come to me first with their requirements! In my business I deal with the customer all the time, whether that is a consultant, business manager or even the IT director. Whatever, they will usually have an understanding of what they need from me in order for them to satisfy their own business needs, although they might not be aware of the latest product offerings. This is why I tend to bring a few technical specialists with me after the initial meeting, so they can demonstrate the product and answer any specific queries that the customer may have (apart from 'How much does it cost?' – that's my job).

IT is much more business-focused than it used to be, which I like, and I tend not to get involved in product configuration options and specifications, but more of how it will help my clients achieve their own business objectives. Luckily, I do understand the products from a technical point of view, as I started off as a computer programmer and then spent a few years as a team leader in a technical support environment before I eventually moved into sales.

The job is very demanding: I have to travel a lot and meet customers at their convenience, not mine – so if that means meeting them at 7 pm on a Friday, then that's when I've got to go. Luckily, I enjoy meeting people and having a good chat about the industry and what they've been up to recently – it all helps build rapport with the customer. The only downside is that the business lunches tend to play havoc with my figure! If I could sum up my role in one sentence, I would say, 'Hard work, but full of perks!'

## IT TRAINER

With the phenomenal growth in the use of IT, the role of the trainer is becoming ever more important. As more and more businesses invest in new IT systems, there is a greater need for staff to be trained to use such systems. Not surprisingly, IT training is an area that is expanding at a particularly high rate compared to other occupational areas within the IT industry. Training can cover all areas of IT, such as hardware, software and networking components, but also many non-technical areas, such as report-writing and presentation skills. The scope of the training itself can vary from course to course, and can range from teaching a small group of people a few simple instructions on a PC to providing classroom-based training for a whole department on the use of a new software product.

The most important skill required for an IT trainer is the ability to communicate effectively. Basically, you must be *understood*. Obviously, you should possess good technical skills, usually in one or two main areas, but general IT skills would be helpful as well. It is worth remembering that you will often be presenting new material to the class for most of the time during a normal day, either explaining the subject to them or helping them solve any problems they might be experiencing. You will need to remain calm, patient and, above all, professional at all times. Not an easy job, especially when your authority might be challenged by some of the smarter students in your class!

Most companies are prepared to take on A-level candidates as well as graduates, usually accepting them into some form of 'train the trainers' programme. If, however, you want to join a professional training company, you may find that most of its trainers or lecturers are freelance IT professionals with specific experience in an IT field, such as project management, testing, UNIX or C.

## Further information

Lots of information on training companies, courses, qualifications and jobs can be found in specialist magazines aimed at training professionals, such as *IT Trainer*, as well as IT magazines such as *Computer Weekly* and *Computing*. Speculative applications may be worthwhile if you can demonstrate specific experience or expert knowledge in a particular area of IT.

## Salary

Starting salaries vary greatly in this area, from £16,000 for the more junior positions, to around £22,000 for new graduates.

## Michelle is a freelance trainer

Having worked for a number of years as a UNIX systems programmer, I realised that I actually enjoyed telling people how the computer system worked more than programming. I suspect this was partly due to the fact that I like meeting people and I consider myself to be a good communicator, especially on technical issues.

For the next few years I worked in the training department of a computer vendor and enjoyed myself immensely. Not only did I have to provide a technical role in planning the course structure and content, but I also had to manage the external contractors we employed for specific courses. Recognising the increasing demand for IT trainers, I then became a freelance contractor, giving me the freedom to train people in many other companies. Working in the M4 corridor, I am now employed by a number of major computer vendors who use freelance contractors, such as Hewlett-Packard and Sun Microsystems. The work is varied, and I do get a lot of free time between courses, which is quite nice in the demanding world of IT. If I had a dislike in being a trainer, it would be the amount of travelling I can sometimes end up doing between customer sites – still, as a contractor, my salary more than makes up for that!

# 7

# Your first steps to success

While this book can prepare you for a career in computing and IT, it cannot guarantee that you will be offered the first job you apply for. Competition in this sector remains tough and employers now expect much more from candidates, both in terms of IT skills and communication skills. The IT profession is very much an industry where personal skills are as important as technical skills. Even if you are an expert C++ programmer, if you can't present IT concepts to business users in a simple way that can be understood, you are likely to find some employers rejecting your CV.

## PLANNING YOUR IT CAREER

If you want to achieve your career aims, you will need to invest time and effort in planning what you want to do. Decisions you take now may well determine how the rest of your career unfolds over the next few years, so take your time and think about your options. The following questions may give you a few ideas of what to consider before embarking upon a career in IT. Answer them as best you can and be honest with yourself:

■   Do you want to be an IT practitioner or an IT user?

- If you want to be an IT practitioner, what role would you enjoy most, for example programmer, analyst, project manager, consultant, games developer or trainer?

- What qualifications and skills do you need to undertake this role?

- What IT skills do you already possess – are they in demand?

- What are you future career plans over the next few years?

- Do you need to gain new skills first?

- Is there an academic or vocational qualification that will help you achieve your career aims?

- Is there a suitable vendor-specific course that may improve your skills?

- Where do you want to work – locally, anywhere in the UK, anywhere in the world?

- Where are you *able* to work – are you mobile, or must you work near where you live?

Armed with this information, you can now decide how best to start your career in IT. You could decide to defer writing job applications until you have gained specific skills or qualifications, as discussed later in the book, or you could decide to enter the industry straight away.

## FINDING A JOB

There are a number of sources you can use to help find a job in computing and IT. The list below shows the main ones, but it is not a definitive list – you must also act on your own initiative:

- computer recruitment fairs;

- national newspapers;

- IT trade magazines;

- Internet job-search sites;

- company Web sites;

- university careers service;

- college careers service;

- job-seekers newspapers;

- local newspapers.

Of these, the two main sources for most IT jobs are the press and the Internet. I make this distinction for one very good reason – an advert placed on a job-hunting Web site will most likely have been placed by a recruitment agency; an advert placed within a professional publication or newspaper will most likely have been placed by the employer directly.

You may think it easier to go through a recruitment agency. Reputable agencies will perform some form of vetting on behalf of their client and you will need to use all your communication skills to convince them that they should recommend your CV to their client. There's more on registering with a recruitment agency, below.

## Local newspapers

Many local and national newspapers advertise vacancies for computing and IT staff, usually under the heading 'Professional' or 'Technical Appointments'.

## National newspapers

The national daily newspapers generally advertise more computing and IT jobs than their local counterparts, but these jobs are primarily aimed at graduates and those IT professionals seeking a more senior role. As you would expect, national newspapers advertise computing and IT vacancies to be found all over the UK, and in many cases, they advertise jobs in other countries too.

## Specialist newspapers

Often published weekly, these large-format newspapers are full of jobs and careers advice, usually for a particular region of the UK (*Yorkshire Jobs*, for instance). While general in nature, catering for many different professions, the jobs are categorised quite well. IT jobs appear under headings such as 'Technical', 'Professional' or 'Computing'.

## Specialist magazines

With an industry as diverse as IT, is it not a complete surprise to find a large number of both general and specialist magazines published specifically for the IT professional. Not all of these include appointments sections, but it is worth paying a visit to the library to have a read of them all the same. The main two magazines that contain job advertisements (as well as lots of other useful information, technical articles and news) are *Computing* and *Computer Weekly*. Both are well established and pride themselves on the staggering number of IT vacancies they publish. They are free to people working in the IT industry, or you can buy them at most newsagents or read them at most libraries.

## The Internet

Using the Internet, you can access the World Wide Web and download information on IT vacancies in the UK and throughout the world. In addition, you can read hundreds of helpful articles on the latest technologies, issues and general career advice. You can obtain access to the Internet from school, college, university or at home (if you have a PC and a modem and Internet connection software). Alternatively, most libraries now have PCs connected to the Internet. See Chapter 9 for useful IT graduate Web sites.

## Registering with a IT recruitment agency

Many organisations advertise directly, but they will often use recruitment agencies to advertise vacancies and perform selection interviews on their behalf, because they do not have the time to handle the hundreds of (often unsuitable) applications they would otherwise receive.

Agencies are very popular with many IT professionals as they are extremely good at getting them a large number of interviews in a relatively short space of time. Agencies work on a commission basis, receiving payment from the recruiting company, usually for every candidate sent for interview plus a bonus payment should they accept the position (usually a percentage of the salary). This does, unfortunately, represent the main problem with using recruitment agencies – they will bend over backwards to find you work if you possess real skills and experience in key areas, but they will soon lose interest in you if you cannot offer them the skills they are seeking. Many of these agencies employ highly skilled, sincere professionals, who will gladly offer career advice and guidance – but they are not charities. To find suitable computer recruitment agencies use the following sources:

▓  IT recruitment Web sites (use an Internet search engine such as www.google.co.uk or try the graduate Web sites mentioned in Chapter 9;

▓  *Computing* and *Computer Weekly* (magazines and Web sites);

▓  *Yellow Pages*, listed under 'Employment Agencies'.

## Approaching employers directly

While it is all very good taking the initiative and contacting employers directly, studies have suggested this is really not worth doing unless you have 'inside knowledge' of a vacancy that has not yet been advertised, or know someone within the organisation who will help with your application.

In one study, over 80 per cent of 'test' applicants who applied directly to the employer were politely informed that, 'There are no vacancies at the present time, but your details will be kept on file.' When the employers were asked three months later about the application details filed, they admitted they did not really have time to sift through any of them, apart from those received in response to a specific advertisement.

If you are confident you can bypass the normal recruitment process, then write a short, simple letter to the IT recruitment manager (or personnel manager), explaining your skills and interests, preferably enclosing a copy of your CV. If possible, find out the name of this manager and address your letter accordingly – it will usually guarantee someone will at least read it. The following points are worth heeding when writing a speculative letter to an employer for any IT vacancy:

- Type your letter (or use a word-processor) on good quality white A4 paper.

- Briefly describe your skills and experience in one paragraph (the rest is on your CV).

- State your availability for an informal discussion or interview should they be interested.

- Leave a contact address and phone number.

- Always enclose an SAE for their reply.

### Further information

Details of IT companies, including contact addresses and the software and hardware they use can be found in *The Computer Users Year Book*, usually available from the reference section of most libraries.

# CAREER ADVICE

Graduate and A-level induction programmes are a welcome introduction into computing and IT for many students, but what about everyone else? Luckily, there are a number of organisations that can find you work and training in IT, regardless of your educational qualifications or financial status.

### Government support services

Most colleges and universities now have their own careers service from where you can obtain career advice and information. In addition, young people in England aged between 13 and 19 can use the government's Connexions service (see Chapter 9 for contact details). In other parts of the UK, Connexions has links with local careers services and can give you contact details for your area. The service aims to provide integrated advice, guidance and access to personal development opportunities for this group and to help them make a smooth transition to adulthood and working life.

Having links with training organisations as well as business, Connexions offers the following services:

- advice on training organisations (colleges, universities and government-backed training companies) that can help you gain IT skills and qualifications;

- advice on studying for qualifications while in work (vocational qualifications);

- information on local and national employers.

## TOP TIPS FOR GETTING INTO THE INDUSTRY

- Be able to *demonstrate* your skills or experience. Have you written a program to solve a problem or fixed a PC either at home or in college? Any practical experience is worth its weight in gold.

- Talk to the employers. They need staff as much as you need a job. Ask the personnel or human resources manager what skills or qualifications they expect potential employees to possess. Showing initiative often creates opportunity.

- Ask your current employer if they would be prepared to send you on an introductory course to learn more about computing and IT (such as the ECDL).

- Many employers now want IT staff to have a broad understanding of *all* the issues affecting IT. Reading the IT trade magazines will help boost your knowledge. Understanding general IT issues will also prepare you for tricky interview questions, such as 'How do you think we can make use of the Internet?'

- Be flexible and open-minded. Seek opportunity. If you are offered a job in IT that is not the one you hoped for, it might be worth taking it to gain experience. See if you can transfer between teams at a later stage or go on a suitable training course.

- Be patient – the IT industry will still be here tomorrow. If you need to do a four-year degree course to achieve your career goal, do it.

- Get as much hands-on experience as you can. PCs are commonplace now – try and get hold of one and teach yourself the basic skills. The Internet is a good example where you can teach yourself the basics of Web design. Many of the skills that are currently in demand are PC-based; for example, competence in Java, C++ and Microsoft Office can be learnt at home.

- There are now many CD-ROM-based training books and manuals to help you gain new skills, many being commonly used within the IT industry. You don't need to buy them: most libraries now stock IT training materials.

# 8

# Training and qualifications

While many successful careers have been built around experience alone, there are a number of good reasons for obtaining training and qualifications in IT:

■ meeting membership criteria for professional IT bodies such as the British Computer Society;

■ to gain accelerated promotion into senior positions;

■ as a 'passport' for moving between IT jobs;

■ to help change careers.

Of course, professional qualifications such as degrees on their own do not guarantee success; training and experience may be needed for roles such as consultant and project manager. However, there is no doubt that a computing qualification provides a potential employer with a recognised assessment of level of commitment and competence.

As well as academic skills, courses such as degrees and higher diplomas can also provide you with many of the 'soft' skills that are highly sought after in industry, such as team-working, communication and presentation skills. An overview of academic qualifications is given in Table 8.1.

**Table 8.1** Academic qualifications

| Academic IT qualifications available | Overview |
|---|---|
| GCSE (or equivalent) | Many schools and colleges offer a GCSE in IT. |
| A level or equivalent | Many schools and colleges also offer an A level in Computer Studies. You will need good GCSE grades to be accepted for an A-level course. |
| GNVQ | General National Vocational Qualification in IT available. |
| S/NVQ | Scottish and National Vocational Qualifications are based on a person's ability to perform a job rather than their level of knowledge. |
| Foundation Modern Apprenticeships/National Traineeships | Innovative training programmes for young people who want to receive work experience, training and qualifications. |
| Advanced Modern Apprenticeship/Modern Apprenticeships | Training programmes that enable young people to work and achieve any one of the IT S/NVQs at Levels 2 and 3 and gain Key Skills. |
| HNC or HND | Higher National Certificate (part-time)/ Higher National Diploma (full-time) courses available in IT and related subjects, such as Business Information Systems and Multi-Media. |
| Degree | University IT courses break down into four subject areas: computer science, information systems, software engineering and artificial intelligence. |
| Postgraduate degree | Typically an MSc or PhD. An MSc IT 'conversion course' is available to non-IT graduates wanting to gain IT skills. |

# ACADEMIC QUALIFICATIONS

## National Vocational Qualifications

National Vocational Qualifications (NVQs, or SVQs in Scotland) in IT are a new and flourishing framework of nationally recognised awards that have been developed jointly by the IT profession and the e-skills National Training Organisation (NTO).

The main aim of an IT NVQ is to provide people with skills that are used and recognised by the IT industry, by adopting a more practical approach to training. Each award is made up of a series of work units that relate to the NVQ topic; the number of units studied depends on the level of NVQ. There are five levels of NVQ:

■ Level 1 provides basic skills, roughly equivalent to GCSEs;

■ Level 2 builds on skills and develops greater understanding;

■ Level 3 assumes more responsibility in the role (equivalent to A levels);

■ Levels 4 and 5 provide a professional (degree level) and postgraduate level of understanding.

*Why should I consider an NVQ?*

■ Not everyone is comfortable sitting exams. NVQs assess your competence at work and rarely involve formal exams.

■ They relate to the real word – a great advantage.

■ NVQs are flexible. There are no time limits, no age limits and no special entry requirements.

NVQs in IT are offered by many colleges and training institutions throughout the UK and are awarded by a number of examinations bodies that all offer their own IT NVQ. For example, the following NVQs are awarded by the City & Guilds of London Institute:

■ Using Information Technology.

■ Use and Support of Information Technology.

■ Operating Information Technology.

■ Software Creation.

■ Install Information Technology Products.

■ Support Users of Information Technology.

■ Information Systems Analysis.

■ Information Systems Design and Programming.

■ Implement Information Technology Solution.

*Further information*

For more information on the NVQ and Modern Apprenticeship programmes, contact:

▓ an IT employer (which might operate an NVQ or Modern Apprenticeship programme);

▓ your local college of further education;

▓ the government support agency (Connexions);

▓ your Local Skills Council (LSC) in England; Training and Employment Agency (T&EA) in Northern Ireland; Local Enterprise Company (LEC) in Scotland;

▓ the e-skills NTO.

## Foundation Modern Apprenticeships (FMAs)/ National Traineeships

FMAs are work-based training programmes leading to, at least, an Level 2 IT NVQ and Key Skills. As this is a work-based qualification, you will receive a wage while you train. FMAs can last up to two years, depending on how much you know before you start, how hard you work, and how much help you get from your employer. FMAs are only available in England and Wales. In Scotland, a similar scheme is available, called *Skillseekers*.

To enrol on an FMA you must be:

▓ aged between 16 and 19;

▓ interested in a career in computing and IT;

▓ able to work and study at the same time;

▓ able to demonstrate the potential to achieve NVQ Level 2 and Key Skills.

*Where will an FMA lead?*

▓ Entry onto a Modern Apprenticeship scheme.

▓ More work experience and an HNC.

▓ Gaining an NVQ Level 3 while at work.

## Modern Apprenticeships

Modern Apprenticeships are work-based training programmes that lead to the achievement of an NVQ Level 3 and Key Skills. They are available for users of IT and for IT professionals and are supported by many IT organisations, including IBM. It is a training programme but also a job, and modern apprentices will be paid while they train. The Modern Apprenticeship in IT has three routes:

1. Using IT.

2. Operating, Installing and Supporting IT Systems.

3. Developing IT Systems.

A Modern Apprenticeship will take up to three years to complete, but like the FMA, you can reduce the time needed in a number of ways.

To enrol as a Modern Apprentice you must be:

▓ aged between 16 and 19;

▓ interested in a career in computing and IT;

▓ able to work and study at the same time;

▓ able to demonstrate the potential to achieve NVQ Level 3 and Key Skills.

### *Where will a Modern Apprenticeship lead?*

▓ Entry onto a degree course.

▓ Entry onto an HND course.

▓ Gaining an NVQ Level 4 in IT.

## HNC/HND

These qualifications are widely recognised in England, Scotland, Wales, Northern Ireland and in some countries overseas. Being vocational in nature they tend to offer practical computing skills rather than academic theory and are widely respected for their relevance to computing occupations within the IT industry. There are many agencies that award HNC/HND qualifications, but the most widely respected and well known is

BTEC (British Technology Education Council), which is now part of Edexcel.

The main BTEC qualifications available are:

- First Certificate/Diploma – age on entry 16+, one-year, equivalent to two GCSEs at grades A–C*. For entry to A levels, BTEC National qualification and NVQ Level 3.

- Advanced GNVQ (General NVQ) – no formal entry requirements, normally two-years, but no real time constraints, equivalent to two A levels.*

- National Certificate/Diploma – no formal entry requirements, three-years part-time/two-years full-time, equivalent to two A levels.*

- Higher National Certificate/Diploma – no formal entry requirements, but any of the following would indicate suitability: one A level, BTEC National qualification, equivalent to a degree.*

*Owing to the vocational nature of BTEC programmes, a direct comparison is not always appropriate. These are the generally accepted equivalents.

## University degrees

There is now a wide variety of computing degrees available from universities that go some way beyond the 'standard' computer science degree, reflecting the importance the industry is placing on new technologies. For example, degrees such as Artificial Intelligence, Cybernetics and Software Engineering are now available, which will qualify you for work within the more specialised fields of the IT industry.

In England, Wales and Northern Ireland degrees normally comprise three-years' full-time study, or four-years' study, including a year's placement in industry (a 'sandwich' degree). In Scotland, an honours degree will typically take four years' full-time study to complete. Remembering that employers are looking for practical skills as well as academic knowledge, a year spent in industry will grab the attention of many IT recruitment managers, and can mean a larger starting salary in some cases.

Entry to higher education can be achieved through courses such as HNC/D, GNVQ Advanced and Modern Apprenticeships, but the most popular route to university is by taking A levels. With one or twoA levels, you can usually apply for an ordinary degree, but for honours degrees, three A levels are normally expected. You do not need mathematics or computing A levels, but you do need to get the highest grades you can as competition for popular degrees is fierce. If, however, you decide to study for a scientific degree, such as computational mathematics or cybernetics, you will normally be expected to have good A-level grades in mathematics or physics.

### The new-style 'Information Management' business degree

Some of the UK's biggest employers are backing a new style of degree that promises to create IT professionals with the business and interpersonal skills needed to become quickly productive in the workplace. The degree will begin at Brighton University in 2004 before rolling out to other UK universities. It addresses employers' concerns that IT graduates can need up to 18 months of coaching before they start making a financial contribution to the business. It also has the potential to cut employers' training costs.

The Information Technology Management BSc, developed by Brighton University with BT, Ford, Norwich Union and other leading employers, will dispense with traditional lectures in favour of teamwork, problem solving and e-learning. Students will spend part of each year in industry, working in groups on real-life IT projects in the sponsoring businesses, where they will learn about the workplace and meet IT managers. IT directors and senior managers from business will give regular seminars. Students will also be trained in presentation, communication and business skills, which they will put into practice with their technical IT skills.

Employers will be involved in the selection process for the programme, and although there are no guaranteed jobs, the firms, including IBM, have made it clear that they are likely to offer jobs to graduates who make a good impression.

Twenty-five places with bursaries from the South of England Development Agency to study at Brighton University's Hastings campus will be offered as part of a local regeneration programme and it is hoped that 10 more universities will adopt similar programmes by 2009.

# PROFESSIONAL AND SPECIALIST QUALIFICATIONS

These are outlined in Table 8.2.

### European Computer Driving Licence (ECDL)

The phenomenal take-up of this qualification is supporting the British Computer Society (BCS) in its mission to raise skill standards and promote the awareness of IT within the workplace. Not surprisingly, the ECDL is proving to be a huge success with employers and employees alike. During 2003 over a million people achieved, or registered for the ECDL IT skills qualification – impressive when you think the ECDL was launched in the UK by the BCS just five years ago. 2004 looks set to be another successful year with 1,600 candidates registering for the Advanced Qualification in January alone.

The ECDL produces clear benefits for those who study for it: not only does it provide people with a qualification that is recognised worldwide, there is also no prior knowledge of IT or computer skills required to join an ECDL training course.

**Table 8.2** Professional and specialist qualifications

| Professional and specialist qualifications available | Overview |
| --- | --- |
| ECDL | European Computer Driving Licence. |
| ISEB | IT certificates and diplomas available from the British Computer Society Information Systems Examination Board (ISEB). |
| City & Guilds Basic Certificate in Computer Programming | Popular exam for direct entry into programming. |
| Royal Society of Arts qualifications | Popular qualifications for pre-college students. |
| Vendor-specific qualifications | Industry-recognised courses available in specific areas of IT. |

Many employers, in both the public and private sectors, use the ECDL to train staff who use IT. Some of these, including IBM, the Bank of England, Sainsbury's, financial services group HSBC and pharmaceuticals giant Pfizer have now adopted the ECDL as a standard. In the public sector, the Cabinet Office is offering civil service staff the opportunity to gain the qualification, as is the NHS and the Ministry of Defence.

Commitment from employers to support the ECDL has been extremely high, which has endorsed the view that this is *the* recognised standard for the training and assessment of computer users worldwide: 3 million people in more than 125 countries have now achieved the qualification or registered to take it.

*ECDL modules*

The ECDL consists of seven modules, each of which must be passed before an ECDL certificate is awarded. The seven modules cover:

- basic IT concepts;
- using the computer and managing files;
- word processing;
- spreadsheets;
- database;
- presentation; and
- information and communication.

Advanced modules are available in word processing and spreadsheets. Full details are available from the British Computer Society; the contact details are in Chapter 9.

## ISEB

ISEB provides industry-recognised qualifications covering all areas of IT. The exams are of an extremely high standard, designed and examined by IT professionals. ISEB is the examinations body of the British Computer Society and ISEB courses are delivered by accredited course providers. Many companies using IT (employing IT practitioners and IT users) already send staff on ISEB courses to help them develop their careers – well over 15,000 people a year are now working for the ISEB certificates and diplomas. The Certificate in Project Management notched up its 5,000th candidate during 2003 and the Business Systems Diploma saw its 1,000th successful candidate.

The ISEB courses are:

- Project management;

- Software testing;

- Data protection;

- Information communications technology;

- Information security;

- Business systems development;

- Service management;

- Programme/project support office;

- Dynamic Systems Development Methodology (DSDM);

- Consultancy practice.

## City & Guilds Basic Certificate in Computer Programming

The City & Guilds (C&G) Institute awards a number of qualifications that are widely recognised and appreciated by IT employers. The C&G Certificate in Computer Programming is a popular choice for many people who want to enter the IT profession directly (or straight from school) as a trainee or junior programmer. Most of the courses offered by the C&G Institute require no formal entry qualifications, although it is better if you possess GCSE English language and mathematics (or the equivalent).

## Royal Society of Arts qualifications

Founded in 1754, the Royal Society of Arts (RSA) provides a number of qualifications covering IT in general as well as specific IT applications. RSA programmes are offered by approved centres, which can be training institutions or colleges of further education. The main RSA qualifications include:

▓ Computer Literacy and Information Technology (CLAIT). A popular, flexible course in IT that is taken annually by over 120,000 candidates, 40 per cent of whom are school pupils. CLAIT is an employable qualification in its own right, but also provides a solid grounding for further study, such as GNVQ, NVQ or A level.

▓ Integrated Business Technology Stage II. A more advanced course integrating a number of IT applications in a simulated office situation, requiring some knowledge of hardware. To enrol, students will need skills at least to CLAIT level.

## Vendor-specific qualifications

In the pursuit of gaining highly productive staff very quickly, some employers now prefer applicants with specific qualifications in IT software and hardware as opposed to the more generic IT qualifications available in colleges and universities. Vendor-specific qualifications are now becoming as important as degrees and diplomas with many companies, as they certify competency in a product that is recognised throughout the world.

All of the major computer vendors and training companies run in-house courses, covering a wide range of topics on many different platforms. As you would expect, the standard of the tuition is extremely high, and as many courses provide 'hands-on' experience in the classroom, these courses are very popular among IT professionals. Before you apply for one of these courses you should think very seriously about cost – they are not cheap and you may find a similar course costing considerably less being run at a local college or university.

### Leading vendor-specific qualifications

▓ Certified Novell Administrator (CNA) – to handle day-to-day administration of an installed Novell networking product, such as Netware.

101

- Certified Novell Engineer (CNE) – installing and upgrading network systems and performing tuning.

- Microsoft Certified Product Specialist (MCPS) – qualified to install, configure and support Microsoft desktop products. MCPSs have considerable knowledge in one of the Microsoft operating systems.

- Microsoft Certified Systems Engineer (MCSE) – qualified to install and support Windows NT and server products. Candidates must pass a total of six exams to achieve certification.

- Certified Java Programmer – gaining knowledge in basic Java programming techniques.

- Certified Java Developer – more in-depth knowledge of Java, including memory management, screen design and graphics. To gain this qualification you must first possess the Certified Java Programmer qualification.

## TRAINING COMPANIES

There are a number or companies that provide a wide range of training programmes, covering all aspects of computing and IT. Many of these companies also run non-technical courses on topics such as communication and team-building skills; see Chapter 9 for details.

# 9

# Useful addresses and further reading

## WHERE TO STUDY

Connexions, the government agency supporting welfare and personal development, can provide details on learning options and course providers for a wide range of qualifications including GCSEs, A levels, RSA, City & Guilds, NVQ, HNC/HND, degree and postgraduate qualifications. For further information Tel 080 800 13219 or go to www.connexions.gov.uk.

### University courses

For details of all university courses and entrance requirements, consult the *University and Colleges Admissions Service Handbook.* For all matters concerning university admission and student loans contact: UCAS, Rosehill, New Barn Lane, Cheltenham, Gloucestershire GL52 3LZ, Tel: 0870 112 2211, Web site: www.ucas.ac.uk.

### Open University degrees

The Open University (OU) specialises in offering a wide range of courses (including degrees) that are completed at home. To obtain an OU degree, you need to accumulate credits in core and supplementary modules over a number of years. For more information on the Open University contact: The Open University, Central Enquiry Service, PO Box 200, Walton Hall,

Milton Keynes MK7 6YZ, Tel: 01908 653 231, Web site: www.open.ac.uk.

## College courses

Many colleges offer good full-time, part-time and/or evening classes, which are often cheap and sometimes free. For general advice on courses (academic and work-based), use the Careers Service, contact e-skills UK, or visit your LSC/LEC/T&EA. e-skills UK is the industry-driven organisation responsible for developing the quality and quantity of professional skills in these sectors. In addition, e-skills UK also has the remit to improve general skills in IT in the UK.

For specific information on colleges and course options, read the *CRAC Directory of Further Education,* published by Hobsons Publishing, available in the reference section of most libraries.

*Contact information*

e-skills UK (for S/NVQ and Modern Apprenticeships), 1 Castle Lane, London SW1E 6DR, Tel: 020 7963 8920, E-mail: info@e-skillsnto.org.uk; Web sites: www.e-skills.com; www.eskillsnto.org.uk/ scotland

General information on Modern Apprenticeships: Web site: www.realworkrealplay.info

ELWa: Web site: www.elwa.org.uk

LEC: Web site: www.hie.co.uk; www.scottish-enterprise.com

T&EA: Web site: www.tea-ni.org.uk

LSC: Web site: www.realworkrealplay.info/lsc

Learndirect helpline (free), for details on courses at local level, Tel: 0800 100 900 (England, Wales and Northern Ireland), or 0808 100 9000 (Scotland), or go to www.learndirect.co.uk.

## City & Guilds of London Institute Study Centres

For details of examinations and approved study centres contact: City & Guilds of London Institute, 1 Giltspur Street, London EC1A 9DD, Tel: 020 7294 2468, Web site: www.city-and-guilds.co.uk

## ISEB qualifications

For details of accredited ISEB course providers, contact the ISEB customer support team, Tel: 01793 417 542 or e-mail: isebenq@hq.bcs.org.uk.

## Centres offering National Vocational Qualifications

For details of colleges and training establishments offering NVQs in IT you must first contact one of the NVQ awarding bodies. Contact the e-skills NTO or one of the following organisations that award NVQs in IT:

British Computer Society, 1 Sandford Street, Swindon SN1 1HJ, Tel: 01793 417 417, Web site: www.bcs.org.uk

City & Guilds of London Institute, 1 Giltspur Street, London EC1A 9DD, Tel: 020 7294 2468, Web site: city-and-guilds.co.uk

National Computing Centre, Oxford House, Oxford Road, Manchester M1 7ED, Tel: 0161 228 6333, Web site: www. ncc.co.uk

Edexcel (formed from the merger of BTEC and London Exams), Head Office, Stewart House, 32 Russell Square, London WC1B 5DN, Customer Services, Tel: 0870 240 9800

National Computing Centre Scotland, Anderson House, 389 Argyle Street, Glasgow G2 8LF, Tel: 0141 204 3725, Web site: edexcel.org.uk

## ECDL

For information, contact the British Computer Society, 1 Sandford Street, Swindon SN1 1HJ, Tel: 01793 417 424, Web site: www.bcs.org/ecdl

## Teaching IT

Graduate Teacher Training Registry, Rosehill, New Barn Lane, Cheltenham, Gloucestershire GL52 3LZ, Tel: 01242 223 707, Web site: www.gttr.ac.uk

Licensed Teacher Scheme, Licensed Teacher Administration Unit, Project Place, 1 Princes Road, Ferndown, Dorset BH22 9JG, Tel: 01202 897 691

Teacher Training in Wales, The National Assembly for Wales, FHE3 Division, Cathays Park, Cardiff CF1 3NQ, Tel: 01222 825 831 or 01222 826 749, Web site: www.wales.gov.uk

Teaching Information Line, Tel: 0845 6000 991

UCAS, Rosehill, New Barn Lane, Cheltenham, Gloucestershire GL52 3LZ, Tel: 0870 112 2211, Web site: www.ucas.ac.uk

*Useful teaching Web sites*

Graduate teacher programme: www.useyourheadteach.gov.uk/routes_into_teaching

Pay and conditions: www.canteach.gov.uk/exitpoints/teacherspay.htm

Financial incentives for teachers: www.canteach.gov.uk/exitpoints/dfes_support.htm

Repayment of teacher's loan scheme: www.useyourheadteach.gov.uk/exitpoints /teachernet_loans.htm

TeacherNet (salary information): www.teachernet.gov.uk/pay

# PROFESSIONAL ASSOCIATIONS

The British Computer Society (BCS), 1 Sandford Street, Swindon SN1 1HJ, Tel: 01793 417 417, Web site: www.bcs.org.uk

The Council of European Professional Informatics Societies (CEPIS), 7 Mansfield Mews, London W1M 9FJ, Tel: 020 7637 5607, Web site: www1.bcs.org.uk

The Engineering Council, 10 Maltravers Street, London WC2R 3ER, Tel: 020 7240 7891, Web site: www.engc.org.uk

The Institute of Data Processing Management (IDPM), IDPM House, Edgington Way, Ruxley Corner, Sidcup, Kent DA14 5HR, Tel: 020 8308 0747, Web site: www.interlink.co.uk/ idpm

# TRAINING ORGANISATIONS

Amdahl UK Education, Beaumont, Old Windsor, Berkshire SL4 2JP, Tel: 01753 833 555, Web site: www.amdahl-education.co.uk

Learning Tree International Ltd, Mole Business Park, Leatherhead, Surrey KT22 7AD, Tel: 01372 364 610 or 0800 282 353, Web site: www.learningtree.co.uk

Microsoft Education, for training in all Microsoft products and MCPS/MCSE certification. Microsoft has a large number of Approved Training Centres where you can obtain training throughout the UK. Web site: www.microsoft.com/uk/skills

Novell UK Education and Training, for all Novell courses including CNA and CNE certification, Tel: 0800 966 196, Web site: www.novell.co.uk

Oracle Education, for training on all Oracle products and general IT skills, Tel: 01344 383 755, Web site: http://education.oracle.com

Sun Educational Services, Sun Microsystems Ltd, Educational Services, Watchmoor Park, Riverside Way, Camberley, Surrey GU15 3YL, Tel: 01276 416 520, Web site: www.sun.co.uk/services/education

# EMPLOYMENT

Contact details for the companies profiled in this book:

Barclays plc, Web site: www.careers.barclays.co.uk

British Airways, Web site: www.britishairways.jobs.com

BT plc, Web site: www.btplc/careerzone

Cap Gemini, Ernst & Young, Web site: www.cgey.co.uk

GlaxoSmithKline, GSK Response Centre; this team is based in the USA so lines are open between 3 pm and 10 pm on 020 8047 4777.

IBM, Recruitment Services, PO Box 41, North Harbour, Portsmouth, Hants PO6 3AU, Web site: www.ibm.co.uk

Intel Ireland Ltd, Personnel Department, Collinstown Industrial Park, Leixlip, County Kildare, Ireland, Tel: 00353 1 606 7000, Web site: www.intel.ie

Pearson Publishing, Web site: pearsonpublishing.co.uk

Syntegra, Tel: 01635 584 135, Web site: www.syntegra.com

Tesco, Web site: www.tesco.com/careers

# USEFUL IT GRADUATE WEB SITES

www.jobs.ac.uk (educational jobs, all levels)

www.graduate-recruitment-jobs.com

www.cwjobs.co.uk *(Computer Weekly)*

www.graduate-recruitment.co.uk

www.grb.uk.com

www.agr.org.uk

www.milkround.com

www.totaljobs.com (professional/graduate IT jobs)

# FURTHER READING

## Specialist computer publications

*Computing/Computer Contractor*, VNU Business Publications, VNU House, 32–24 Broadwick Street, London W1A 2HG, Tel: 020 7316 9000, Web site: www.vnunet.com

*Computer Weekly/Freelance Informer*, Reed Business Publishing, Quadrant House, The Quadrant, Sutton, Surrey SM2 5AS, Tel: 01444 441 212, Web site: www. computerweekly.com

*The Computer Users Year Book*, Learned Information (Europe) Ltd, Woodside, Hinksey Hill, Oxford OX1 5BE, Tel: 01865 388 000, Web site: www.learned.co.uk

## Kogan Page testing and job search books

*Testing books*

*Aptitude, Personality and Motivation Tests*, Barrett, 2004, ISBN: 0 7494 4178 9

*The Aptitude Test Workbook*, Barrett, 2003, ISBN: 0 7494 3788 X

*How to Master Psychometric Tests,* Parkinson, 2000, ISBN: 0 7494 3420 1

*How to Pass Numeracy Tests*, Tolley and Thomas, 2000, ISBN: 0 7494 3437 6

*How to Pass Numerical Reasoning Tests*, Smith, 2003, ISBN: 0 7494 3958 0

*How to Pass Professional Level Psychometric Tests*, al-Jajjoka, 2001, ISBN: 0 7494 3647 6

*How to Pass Verbal Reasoning Tests*, Tolley and Thomas, 2000, ISBN: 0 7494 3436 8

*How to Succeed at an Assessment Centre*, Tolley and Wood, 2001, ISBN: 0 7494 3478 3

*IQ and Psychometric Tests*, Carter, 2004, ISBN: 0 7494 4118 6

*The Times Book of IQ Tests – Book 3*, Russell and Carter, 2003, ISBN: 0 7494 3959 9

*Job search aids*

*Britain's Top Employers*, Corporate Research Foundation, 2003, ISBN: 0 7494 3933 5

*Great Answers to Tough Interview Questions*, Yate, 2001, ISBN: 0 7494 3552 6

*How You Can Get That Job!*, Corfield, 2002, ISBN: 0 7494 3894 0

*Net that Job! Using the World Wide Web to develop your career and find work*, Krechowiecka, 2000, ISBN: 0 7494 3314 0

*Preparing Your Own CV*, Corfield, 2003, ISBN: 0 7494 3839 2

*Readymade CVs*, Williams, 2000, ISBN: 0 7494 3321 3

*Readymade Job Search Letters*, Williams, 2000, ISBN: 0 7494 3322 1

*Successful Interview Skills*, Corfield, 2002, ISBN: 0 7494 3892 4

For further information on Kogan Page publications, go to www.kogan-page.co.uk.

# Appendix 1

# Recruitment tests

There are still organisations that do not use any form of aptitude tests or assessment procedures to select potential IT recruits, but doing so is becoming common practice among graduate employers.

IT aptitude tests assess the suitability of candidates for a career in the IT industry. As computing theory is based around logic, so too are many IT aptitude tests. They don't test specific IT skills or knowledge, and you certainly won't be asked to explain the fundamentals of Java or the benefits of structured programming. However, they will test your mental prowess and your ability to manipulate information or objects. Quite how relevant aptitude tests are is still open to debate, but that is not the issue here; you may be expected to complete one or more aptitude tests when you apply for graduate IT positions and you will need to be prepared for them.

## PROGRAMMING TESTS

A job-related tutorial test, the Berger Aptitude for Programming Test (B-APT) requires the candidate to learn a simple hypothetical programming language and use it to solve a series of problems. Candidates must understand the rules of the language and use it to write short programs in a test booklet. The reasoning behind this is fairly simple: you can master any programming language if you can understand the rules upon which it is based. A good programmer is one who, given the rules, can program in any language!

# CASE STUDY TESTS

These differ from other types of aptitude tests in that they are relevant, practical and really test your ability to extract key information and issues from case study material. You will, in most cases, be expected to have a good understanding of IT and how it can benefit organisations – even if you are a non-IT graduate. Case study tests are used to assess candidates for analysis, consultancy and support roles; the following example is typical of the format used for business analysis and consultancy roles.

## SUNNYTHWAITE CONSTABULARY

### Background

A number of interviews have taken place between a principal IT consultant and senior staff within Sunnythwaite Constabulary. Senior police officers have been concerned for some time that their crime recording process is neither effective nor efficient. They are thinking they need to improve the quality of the process and automate where possible. You have been given a copy of the notes made from these interviews.

Interview notes from meetings held with Sunnythwaite Constabulary:

*Sunnythwaite City Constabulary comprises 21 Operational Control Units (OCUs) with geographic responsibility for managing police operations and crimes. In total, approximately 365,000 crimes are recorded each year across all OCUs. Some but not all may have been reported previously as 'incidents' via Command and Control, for example if an officer notices that a car has been broken into and radios in but the* owner has not yet returned (in which case a crime cannot be reported). Alternatively a crime may be reported directly by a victim to a police station, bypassing Command and Control.

For each crime reported, a paper-based crime report is filled in, either at one of the OCU operations centres, or by a police officer at the scene of the crime. The paper reports are then sent to the OCU inputting section for data-entry into the IT system, POLICE-IT, typically by civilian staff.

Further steps in the process take place, for example where the crime form is reviewed and validated. This process is crucial to the crime recording process as the reviewers need to make sure the form contains enough information to help solve the crime and that the codes allocated to the crime (as required by the Home Office) are correct for the nature of the crime. The reviewers may have to send the crime form back to the reporting police officer if some details are not complete (this usually means the form is sent via the internal postal system, or in some cases via the Royal Mail). The Constabulary will chase OCUs for reports that have not been satisfactorily filled in within seven days, which is one of a number of key performance indicators used to measure the performance of the Constabulary.

An OCU reviewer may sometimes notice similarities between two crime reports, eg same description of offender, if they had also screened the previous crime. However, this will not happen if screened by another officer of if the crime was committed in an adjacent OCU.

Each OCU has on average four inputters and two police officers reviewing, handling 70 crimes reports per day. This equates to 126 staff for the whole force.

Paperwork handling represents a significant amount of an officer's working shift. Depending on the type of crime, an officer can spend from 20 minutes to 2.5 hours on the process.

*The current procedures are not popular with officers. They are seen as diverting valuable and limited time and energy away from fighting crime, with a knock-on effect on morale.*

*A key objective of any investigation in this area is to look for ways to reduce wasted time and focus more of the available resources on reducing crime in the West Midlands.*

*Attempts have been made to redesign the crimes form, but it remains 'general purpose' by its nature and lacks pertinent questions for specific crimes. In cases of car theft, for example, the owner should be asked if they smoke, and if not, when the car is recovered it will be checked for cigarette butts and a DNA test will be done. 'Solvability factors' such as these help Sunnythwaite decide how a case should be progressed. They also aid the investigation and help to ensure that all possible correct evidence is acquired before submission to the court, eg CCTV clips.*

*The process is very dependent on the physical paperwork and its movement from police officer to satellite station, OCU, inputters, screeners, back to officer, etc. It is also very dependent on the knowledge and experience of particular administration staff and officers. Input staff can have a high turnover, which keeps average skill levels lower, and results in poorer data quality and more work by the screeners.*

*Delays can invariably occur at every step, eg:*

- *paperwork moving between locations;*

- *waiting to be input;*

- *waiting to be reviewed;*

- *having to be returned for more information to the reporting officer, who may be on leave or sick.*

*Data entry errors occur at inputting – even basic poor spelling of an address by one inputter was witnessed.*

*If inputters or screeners 'correct' what an officer has written, this is rarely communicated back to them or their supervising officer. This lack of feedback does not assist officer training. Sometimes the 'correction' may in fact be in error, as the officer knows the fuller context of the crime and other factors. Crimes can therefore be misreported.*

*When officers visit the victim, the emphasis is sometimes seen as on completing the paperwork rather than investigating the crime. Time is spent filling in name, address, etc when often this is already known via Command and Control. If the process could be changed, it is hoped that more time could be spent on collecting evidence and detection while the officer is at the scene and locality, including talking with neighbours, etc.*

### Brief

You have to provide a review of the operations at Sunnythwaite Constabulary, identifying key problems with a view to recommending where IT might be used to help improve the quality of the overall crime recording process. In addition, you have been asked to provide a provisional, high-level model for automating their process, using any IT technologies you think are appropriate.

As a guide, the consultant has categorised the key issues as being:

- data quality (eg errors on crime form);
- functionality (eg the current crime form is too general and does not provide enough information on specific crimes);
- process issues (eg consistency, bottlenecks, constraints, resourcing).

What would you recommend in your report and why?

# PSYCHOMETRIC TESTS

These are by far the most popular type of computer aptitude tests and are used by many employers as part of their graduate recruitment and selection programme. There are lots of different types of reasoning tests available, but IT employers in particular tend to use the five types of tests shown in Table A.1.

**Table A.1**   Types of reasoning test

| Test type | Overview |
| --- | --- |
| Verbal reasoning | Selecting and manipulating words to satisfy questions. |
| Numerical reasoning | Selecting and manipulating numbers to satisfy questions. |
| Diagrammatic | Selecting and manipulating shapes to satisfy questions. |
| Spatial | Ability to satisfy questions by rotating shapes. |
| High-level programming | Many types. Most popular tests concern understanding of the syntax rules for a hypothetical high-level programming language. |

Below are some brief examples of three common types of psychometric test: numerical, diagrammatic and high-level programming. The practice tests have been taken from *How to Pass Professional Level Psychometric Tests*, al-Jajjoka, 2001, Kogan Page, ISBN: 0 7494 3647 6.

## Numerical reasoning

### Problem solving

This test requires, in addition to knowledge of mathematical principles, an understanding of the fundamentals of algebra and arithmetic.

1.  How much will it cost to build a wall round a house that is 25 metres long and 75 metres wide, if the cost of 50 centimetres is £10?

    A            B            C
    £4,000     £40,000     £400

2.  It costs a publisher $n$ pounds for each book to publish the first 1,000 books; extra books cost $n/6$ pounds each. How many pounds will it cost to publish 7,000 books?

    A            B            C
    7,000$n$     2,000$n$     5,000

3.  The distance between London and Hull is 300 miles. An Intercity train travels at 120 miles per hour from London to Hull. The train then goes back to London. If the total journey

time was 4 hours and 30 minutes, what was the average speed of the Intercity train on the way back to London?

| A | B | C |
|---|---|---|
| 160 mph | 140 mph | 150 mph |

4. At weekends the local bowling club charges each person a flat rate of $n$ pounds for up to 3 hours and $1/9n$ for each hour or fraction of an hour after the first 3 hours. How much does it cost for 2 people to go for 6 hours and 25 minutes at the weekend?

| A | B | C |
|---|---|---|
| $6/9n$ | $26/9n$ | $13/9n$ |

5 John bought £3,000 worth of stock in company X. He sold 2/3 of his stock after the value doubled, then sold the remaining stock at 4 times its purchase price. What was the total profit on the stock of company X?

| A | B | C |
|---|---|---|
| £3,000 | £4,000 | £5,000 |

## Interpretation of graphs and data

The ability to calculate and measure statistical information is very important in many IT roles, especially within business analysis and consultancy. See Figure A.1 for data.

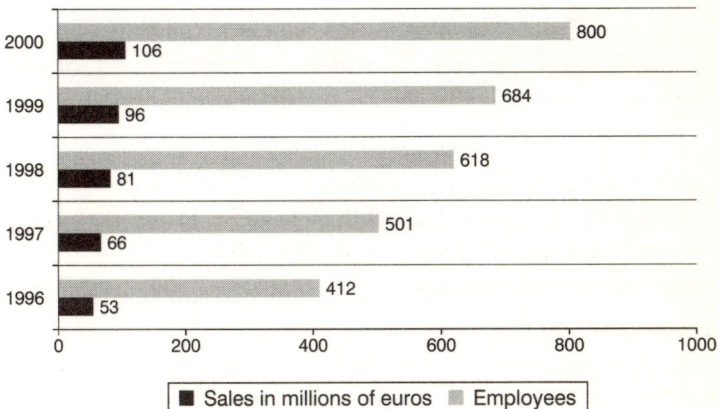

**Figure A.1** Continuous growth of sales and staff

1. By approximately what percentage did total staff numbers change from 1996 to 2000?

   A   B   C
   387  94%  90%

2. By what percentage did the total profit change from 1996 to 2000?

   A   B       C
   100%  53 million euros 50%

3. If the number of employees in 2001 has increased by 25 per cent over 2000, what was the total number of new recruits in 2001 compared with 2000?

   A   B   C
   200  1,000  1,200

4. Between 1996 and 2000, which years showed the smallest and largest staff profit numbers, respectively?

   A       B      C
   1996 and 2000  1999 and 1996  1999 and 1998

5. If 1 euro = £0.65, then the profit in 1999 was approximately

   A       B      C
   £6,240,000  £62.4 million  624,000,000 euros

6. If there are 300 additional recruits in 2001 and the average growth of sales and staff remains constant, how much greater would the total sales volume (in euros) for 2001 be?

   A       B      C
   £39.75 million  3,975,000 euros  39,750,000 euros

## Diagrammatic reasoning

*Spatial concepts*

In this test, you are often provided with the net (outline) of a benchmark unfolded box with a different pattern on each side. Your task is to build a three-dimensional image of the box and compare views of this box from different angles to another set of boxes. You must decide which of these views matches the benchmark view and mark your answer accordingly.

Now look at Figure A.2 and see how many of the associated questions in Figure A.3 you can complete in three minutes. To help you with this exercise I have provided the three-dimensional solution.

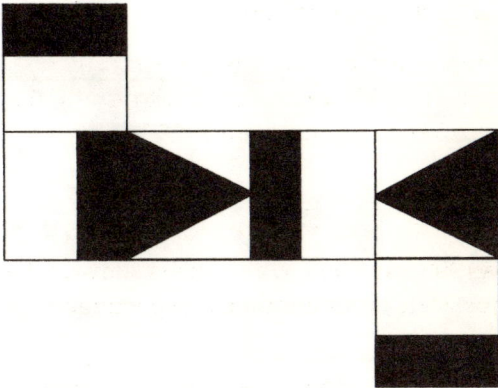

**Figure A.2** Net

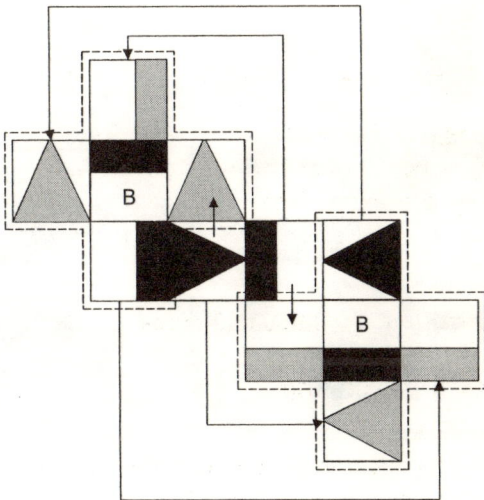

**Figure A.2** Three-dimensional solution

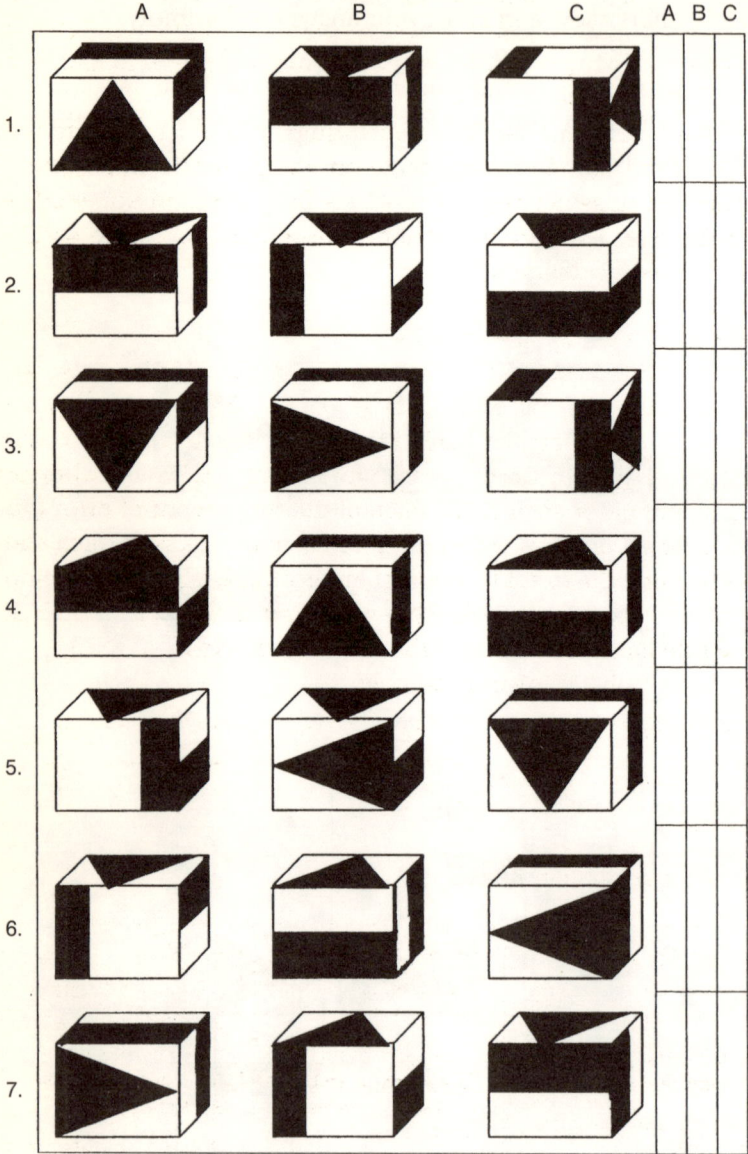

**Figure A.3**

# High-level programming tests

The translation of a high-level programming language such as C, Java or COBOL into machine instructions a computer can understand is performed using a computer program called a compiler.

The test in this section is one where you must perform the role of the compiler, identifying errors in a mock-up program. This test does not require previous programming knowledge as the rules used are likely to be different to those used within software development.

## *Compiler checking by tracking error*

In this test you will find a mock-up of unstructured programming lines taken from a C look-alike language, which contain many errors. The errors have been identified and categorised into three types: syntax error (SE), logical error (LE) and other error (OE). Each of the three types of error has its own set of rules. Using these rules, your task is to trace and determine the exact location of an error in each programming line and then identify the type of error it is, ie SE, LE or OE. If no rule has been broken, cross the column No Error (NE).

Look at the following example:

|  |  | SE | LE | OE | NE |
|---|---|---|---|---|---|
| 1. | Printf ("\n Maximum and minimum of the 3 numbers |  |  |  |  |

Now look at the following set of rules:

| SE rules: | LE rules: | OE rules: |
|---|---|---|
| **A** Lines must end in a colon (:). | **A** Division by zero is not allowed. | **A** Lines must begin with semi-colon (;). |
| **B** Number must be between stars, eg, *7*. | **B** All arithmetical expressions must be written in upper case eg X = Y + 7; | **B** Double quotation (") can only be used with Printf statement. |
| **C** All characters may be used except @, $. | X1/Y1 | **C** Rule A from SE and OE does not apply on the opening brace [. |

As you can see, rules A and B in SE have been broken; the line should end in a colon and the number, ie 3, should be between stars. No rules are broken in LE. Rule A has been broken in OE, because of the missing semi-colon at the beginning of the line. Therefore, you should cross the SE and OE columns, as shown below:

|  | | SE | LE | OE | NE |
|---|---|---|---|---|---|
| 1. | Printf ("\n Maximum and minimum of the 3 numbers | X | | X | |

Now try the following exercise. See how many you can complete in 10 minutes, then compare your results with the answers given at the end of this appendix.

|  | | SE | LE | OE | NE |
|---|---|---|---|---|---|
| 1. | ;Include<stdio.h>, | | | | |
| 2. | ;Include <math.h>: | | | | |
| 3. | #define (NST): | | | | |
| 4. | ;double a1b1/x1, Y3 | | | | |
| 5. | ;main (11Maxim@), | | | | |
| 6. | ;{ | | | | |
| 7. | ;Printf("na="); X/*0*=Y: | | | | |
| 8. | ;Scanf(7)%1f, &a): | | | | |
| 9. | ,Printf ("%f,*10*);X | | | | |
| 10. | ,(\* Calculate ymax @ Ymax, "9"): | | | | |
| 11. | XM=0.5+X2(Y1–Y2): | | | | |
| 12. | ;MAX=OR+T: | | | | |
| 13. | ;Printf("\n X=8%, Y=8%8+61), | | | | |
| 14. | } | | | | |
| 15. | ;Void=X1/Y1+7 | | | | |
| 16. | {: | | | | |
| 17. | ;X1=A+0.5(B–A(NST): | | | | |
| 18. | ;Y1=x(R1): | | | | |
| 19. | If (y1=y2) Then Y1=8+x | | | | |
| 20. | Printf("n Interest Rate"); | | | | |
| 21. | :For (c=1; c <=20/0;++ c); | | | | |
| 22. | ;L=0.01+n, | | | | |

| | | SE | LE | OE | NE |
|---|---|---|---|---|---|
| 23. | ,Return: | | | | |
| 24. | ,Scanf("a, @/B): | | | | |
| 25. | ;Maximum (x,y): | | | | |
| 26. | ;While (N/*0*=X+Y) Then X=Y: | | | | |
| 27. | For (count=1; count<=n;count=1+n) | | | | |
| 28. | ,Func1 (int n): | | | | |
| 29. | ;int y=X: | | | | |
| 30. | ;X/0=Y: | | | | |
| 31. | ;Return: | | | | |
| 32. | } | | | | |
| 33. | ,Int Funct1 (inta1): | | | | |
| 34. | ;(int funct2 (X+Y=2)): | | | | |
| 35. | ,B=F($): | | | | |
| 36. | ,Return; | | | | |
| 37. | ;/initialise and read in a value for /: | | | | |
| 38. | ; While x=y calculate the average : | | | | |
| 39. | ; AVERAGE=X+T–Y: | | | | |
| 40. | ;Read in the number: | | | | |
| 41. | ;For "(c=x; c<=n c=n+x)": | | | | |

# ANSWERS

## Problem solving

1. A; 2. B; 3. C; 4. B; 5. C.

## Interpretation of graphs and data

1. B; 2. A; 3. A; 4. B; 5. B; 6. C.

## Spatial concepts

1. A; 2. C; 3. B; 4. C; 5. C; 6. B; 7. C.

## Compiler checking by tracking error

| | | |
|---|---|---|
| 1. SE | 2. NE | 3. OE |
| 4. SE, LE | 5. SE | 6. OE |
| 7. LE | 8. SE | 9. SE, OE |

10. SE, OE
11. SE, OE
12. NE
13. SE
14. NE
15. SE, LE
16. LE
17. SE
18. LE
19. SE, LE
20. SE, OE
21. SE, LE, OE
22. SE, LE
23. OE
24. SE, OE
25. NE
26. SE, LE
27. SE, LE, OE
28. OE
29. LE
30. SE, LE
31. NE
32. NE
33. OE
34. SE
35. SE, OE
36. SE, OE
37. NE
38. LE
39. NE
40. NE
41. LE, OE

# Appendix 2

# The likely IT roles and their purpose within the SDLC

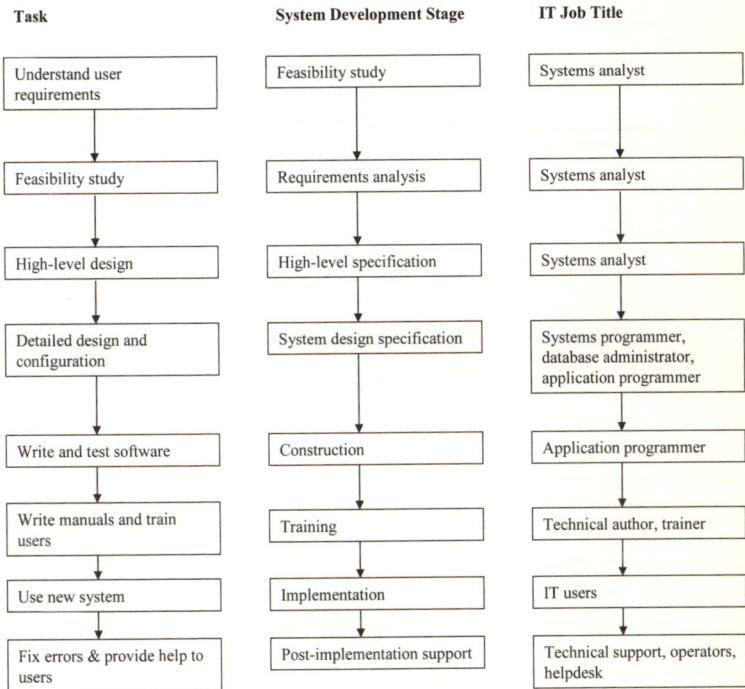

| Task | System Development Stage | IT Job Title |
|---|---|---|
| Understand user requirements | Feasibility study | Systems analyst |
| Feasibility study | Requirements analysis | Systems analyst |
| High-level design | High-level specification | Systems analyst |
| Detailed design and configuration | System design specification | Systems programmer, database administrator, application programmer |
| Write and test software | Construction | Application programmer |
| Write manuals and train users | Training | Technical author, trainer |
| Use new system | Implementation | IT users |
| Fix errors & provide help to users | Post-implementation support | Technical support, operators, helpdesk |

# Glossary

**artificial intelligence (AI)**   Computer systems that perform functions that would require intelligence if performed by humans, eg reasoning and decision-making.

**assembler**   A low-level programming language that can be converted into machine code. Assembler language is often used for applications where speed is important, such as games programming.

**business process re-engineering**   Radically improving the business by using IT to improve performance and cut costs.

**C**   A high-level programming language developed at Bell Laboratories in the USA. UNIX is written in C.

**C++**   A more advanced version of the C programming language, which is used for object-oriented program development.

**CD-ROM**   Compact Disk-Read Only Memory – a small plastic disk that is used as a high-capacity storage medium. A CD-ROM player is the device that enables a computer to read the CD-ROM.

**COBOL**   Common Ordinary Business-Oriented Language – an old but very popular programming language used for writing business applications.

**console**   A computer terminal that allows a computer operator to access the computer system, usually in order to issue operating system commands.

**database**   A set of related files that can store text, images, sound and video. Traditionally, databases are used when access is required to large amounts of information, as in stock-control systems or customer account databases.

**distributed computing**   Sharing many computers that are connected together over a network.

**DVD**   Digital Versatile Disk – originally called the Digital Video Disk, a DVD is a type of optical disk similar to a CD, but capable of storing much more information. DVD technology is used by the film industry to store video information and is expected to eventually replace videotapes.

**ethernet**   A local area network protocol (a set of rules which determine how data should be transmitted and received across a LAN).

**expert system**   Software that applies the knowledge of a human expert in a particular field to help diagnose problems.

**high-level language**   A programming language that allows the programmer to write programs using English-like statements (as in COBOL). A separate operation is then performed to translate the program into instructions the computer will understand.

**HTML**   HyperText Markup Language – the document format used on the World Wide Web. Web pages that can be downloaded from the Web are written in HTML.

**Internet**   An international wide-area network connecting together many local networks, providing electronic mail and file-transfer facilities.

**intranet**   A term given to a local or secure Internet, eg a network that exists within a company for use by its employees.

**Jackson Structured Programming (JSP)**   A popular method of writing and designing structured computer programs, developed by Michael Jackson.

**Java**   A high-level computer programming language developed by Sun for writing Internet and Intranet applications.

**LAN**   Local Area Network – a system of connected computer terminals and devices that are within a short distance of each other, eg a series of PCs linked together in the IT department of an organisation.

**microchip**   An electronic circuit used in the assembly of microcomputers etched onto a silicon semiconductor (or 'chip').

**midrange computer**   A medium-sized computer system or server.

**modem**   A device that allows computer data to be transmitted over telephone lines.

**monitor**   A visual display unit (VDU) or screen, used to display high-quality text and graphics on a computer.

**MVS**   Multiple Virtual Storage – a popular (and very powerful) IBM mainframe operating system.

**online**   Connected to and under the control of a computer; available for immediate use. For example, if you connect to the Internet, you are online when you make the connection to the modem and provide a username and password.

**operating system**   A series of programs that control the basic functions of a computer system, such as input/output, memory allocation and file handling.

**PC**   Personal Computer – a general term relating to a microcomputer.

**psuedo-code**   English-like sentences that are used in program design to describe the operation of the program.

**real-time**   A computer system that processes events as they happen, allowing decisions to be made that could influence those events (eg a missile guidance system).

**RISC**   Reduced Instruction Set Computer – a computer architecture that reduces chip complexity by using simpler instructions.

**scanner**   A device that 'reads' a printed page and converts it into a digital image on a computer.

**server**  A computer on a network that provides services used by other computers in the network (eg a mail server).

**software engineering**  A computing field covering all aspects of software development. Software engineering taught in universities often relates to the *science* of writing and testing programs.

**SSADM**  A popular systems analysis and design methodology.

**token ring**  A popular type of LAN architecture in which a computer connected to the network can only transmit data when it is in possession of a token.

**transaction**  A general term usually relating to any single action that is performed in a database (eg deleting a record).

**UNIX**  A popular multi-user operating system developed by AT&T Bell Laboratories that runs on almost any computer, from a PC to a mainframe.

**virus**  A program that attaches to a computer system and then spreads itself to other files or computers on the network, often corrupting them in the process.

**WAN**  A network that connects computers over large distances using high-speed telephone lines, radio and satellites.

**World Wide Web**  An Internet facility that links Web pages together, whether they exist on one server locally, or many servers around the world.

# Index

Page references in *italics* indicate tables or figures.

# Also published by Kogan Page

*Also published by Kogan Page*

*Readymade CVs*
Lynn Williams, 2004, 0 7494 4274 3

*Readymade Job Search Letters*
Lynn Williams, 2004, 0 7494 4277 8

*Test Your Own Aptitude*
Jim Barrett, 2003, 0 7494 3887 8

The above titles are available from all good bookshops. To obtain further information, please contact the publisher at the address below:

Kogan Page Limited
120 Pentonville Road
London N1 9JN
United Kingdom
Tel: +44 (0) 20 7278 0433
Fax: +44 (0) 20 7837 6348
www.kogan-page.co.uk